T0381464

HEALING HEARTS: EMBRACING SACRIFICE FOR PERSONAL GROWTH

Dr. Mark A. McConnell

authorHOUSE®

AuthorHouse™
1663 Liberty Drive
Bloomington, IN 47403
www.authorhouse.com
Phone: 833-262-8899

Published by AuthorHouse 03/13/2025

ISBN: 979-8-8230-4385-4 (sc)
ISBN: 979-8-8230-4384-7 (e)

Library of Congress Control Number: 2025902970

Print information available on the last page.

CONTENTS

FOREWORD

—

Life in and of itself is a journey; on this journey, we will encounter many things and experiences along the way. It has its ebbs and lows, but how we handle things or navigate through them largely determines the outcome. It has been said that our culture and context help to shape our character and worldview. Worldview refers to what we believe, practice, and what shapes our convictions. I believe that included in this development are the various experiences that come along life's journey, whether they are disappointments, victories, failures, brave or scary moments, successes, highs, or lows, they shape and develop who we are in the present. It is an honor to write this forward for Dr. Mark A. McConnell because I have known him for years, I have seen his life close up, and I have watched him from afar. Everything that he has encountered on his journey was not only faced courageously, but it has made him the man, preacher, and pastor that he is today. I am certain that his growth and development have not been suspended, there is more to come.

A Journey of Sacrifice and Renewal gives us a glimpse of what Dr. McConnell has experienced at a critical point on his journey. We are shown how to live through a situation that could have possibly had a different outcome. However, because it was championed by his faith and trust that God would see him through, McConnell's life is a testament to the fact that no matter what comes on the journey you can face it and overcome it. Yes, there was the initial shock, reflection, emotional effect, mental anguish, a test of faith, and extreme concern, but coming out on the other side gave him renewed strength. This book is a mirror to those who read it because it is an example of how we should embrace everything that we may encounter on our journey. Not just embrace it, but allow ourselves to welcome all that comes our way to ensure personal growth and development.

We celebrate the transparency that Dr. McConnell shares in this writing because it gives us hope. It is a reminder to all that if we trust God and remain faithful, victory is waiting for us on the other side. Let us embrace the ride and enjoy the journey as we peer into this living epistle of one's life.

Dr. Rickey L. Lawson Sr.
Senior Pastor
Pilgrim Missionary Baptist Church
Columbus, Ohio

Introduction

A Journey of Sacrifice and Renewal

Opening Narrative

I still vividly remember the day I received the diagnosis. The room felt unbearably silent as the doctor explained the severity of the blockages in all three of my major arteries. My heart, both literally and metaphorically, was failing me. The options were stark and unforgiving: face certain death or undergo a life-saving surgery that required a significant personal sacrifice.

The decision to harvest veins from my left leg to save my heart was not one made lightly. It felt as though I was sacrificing a part of myself to preserve the most vital aspect of my being. As the surgeon prepared for the procedure, I grappled with fear, uncertainty, and a profound sense of gratitude for the second chance I was about to receive.

Post-Surgery Realization

Waking up from surgery, the first thing I noticed was the intense swelling in both of my legs. My left leg, the donor site, was especially swollen—an undeniable reminder of the veins that had been sacrificed to heal my heart. The physical discomfort was palpable, but beneath it lay an emotional and spiritual awakening. This swelling symbolized the sacrifices we often make for our well-being, echoing the profound sacrifices that shape our lives.

Emotional Impact and Faith

As I navigated the days following my surgery, I found solace in my faith. The story of Jesus's ultimate sacrifice on the rugged cross resonated deeply with me. While my personal sacrifice was different in scale and purpose, it mirrored the themes of selflessness, renewal, and hope that are central to my faith. This journey became not just a physical healing process but a spiritual one as well, intertwining personal growth with divine inspiration.

Purpose of the Book

This book is a testament to the power of sacrifice in the pursuit of healing and personal growth. It draws from my own experiences and the profound lessons found in faith, particularly the story of Jesus's sacrifice and resurrection. My hope is that by sharing my journey, others will find inspiration to embrace their own sacrifices, overcome challenges, and achieve meaningful transformation in their lives.

How to Use This Book

Each chapter delves into different aspects of sacrifice and healing, blending personal anecdotes with spiritual reflections and practical exercises. I encourage you to engage with the exercises, reflect on the questions posed, and allow the stories and scriptures to guide your own journey toward healing and growth.

CHAPTER 1

Understanding Sacrifice

The Essence of Sacrifice

Sacrifice is a profound and universal concept that transcends cultures, religions, and personal experiences. At its core, sacrifice involves giving up something valuable for the sake of something greater. Whether it's time, resources, relationships, or even parts of ourselves, sacrifice is often a necessary step toward achieving meaningful growth and healing.

In many ways, sacrifice is the foundation upon which we build resilience and character. It teaches us patience, selflessness, and the importance of prioritizing long-term well-being over immediate gratification. Through sacrifice, we learn to let go of what no longer serves us, paving the way for new opportunities and personal transformation.

Personal Example: My Medical Sacrifice

In my own life, the decision to undergo surgery and sacrifice veins from my left leg was a profound act of selflessness. This sacrifice was not for others but for my own survival and well-being. It required me to let go of a part of myself to preserve my heart, highlighting the personal nature of sacrifice in the face of dire circumstances.

The day I walked into the hospital, I was overwhelmed with a mix of emotions—fear, uncertainty, and a glimmer of hope. The sterile environment, the hushed tones of the medical staff, and the gravity of the situation made it clear that this was a pivotal moment in my life. The surgeon explained that without the procedure, my heart would eventually fail, leading to certain death. Harvesting veins from my left leg to create bypasses for my blocked arteries was the only viable option to save my life.

As I lay on the operating table, the reality of what I was about to do sank in. I was about to give up a part of myself to save my heart. The thought was both terrifying and liberating. Terrifying because it meant enduring pain and a lengthy recovery, and liberating because it offered me a chance at life.

This medical sacrifice was not just a physical loss but also an emotional and spiritual one. It forced me to confront my fears, reassess my priorities, and deepen my reliance on faith. The process was grueling, both physically and emotionally, but it was a necessary step toward healing and personal growth.

Biblical Sacrifices: The Ultimate Example

In Christian faith, the ultimate example of sacrifice is found in Jesus Christ's willingness to lay down His life on the rugged cross for the salvation of mankind. His sacrifice was not just a personal act but a divine one, intended to offer redemption and eternal life to all humanity. This unparalleled act of love and selflessness serves as a profound inspiration for believers, illustrating the transformative power of sacrifice.

Jesus's sacrifice was rooted in unconditional love and obedience to the Father's will. He endured immense suffering, rejection, and ultimately death, all for the sake of humanity's salvation. His resurrection three days later symbolizes victory over death and the promise of new life for all who believe.

This divine sacrifice sets the standard for all acts of giving and selflessness. It teaches us that true sacrifice involves giving something of great value, often at significant personal cost, for the benefit of others or for a higher purpose.

Honoring the Ultimate Sacrifice

While my personal sacrifice represents a significant and meaningful commitment to my own healing and growth, it is essential to recognize that Jesus's sacrifice surpasses all others in its purpose and scope. Jesus gave Himself for the salvation of all, an act of divine love and grace that sets the foundation for our faith and understanding of true sacrifice.

In honoring Jesus's sacrifice, we are reminded of the depth of love and commitment required to make meaningful sacrifices. It serves as a beacon guiding us to live selflessly, to prioritize others' well-being, and to seek purpose beyond our immediate desires.

Common Misconceptions About Sacrifice

Understanding sacrifice requires dispelling several common misconceptions that often cloud our perception of what true sacrifice entails.

1. **Sacrifice is Always Negative:**

    o **Misconception:** Many perceive sacrifice as losing something valuable, leading to feelings of loss and regret.

    o **Reality:** While sacrifice can involve loss, it can also lead to positive outcomes such as growth, healing, and newfound strength. Sacrifices made with intention and purpose can transform challenges into opportunities for development.

    o **Expanded Insight:** Consider the act of giving up a stressful job to pursue a more fulfilling career path. While it involves uncertainty and initial loss, the long-term benefits often include greater satisfaction, personal growth, and improved well-being.

2. **Sacrifice Requires Extreme Measures:**

    o **Misconception:** People often believe that only grand gestures qualify as sacrifices.

    o **Reality:** Sacrifices come in various forms and magnitudes. Small, consistent sacrifices can accumulate and have a significant impact over time. It's not always about the magnitude but the intention and impact of the sacrifice.

o **Expanded Insight:** Simple acts like setting aside time each day for prayer or meditation, or choosing to listen instead of speaking in moments of conflict, are forms of sacrifice that contribute to personal and relational growth.

3. **Sacrifice Must Be Solitary:**

o **Misconception:** Sacrifices are often viewed as solitary endeavors, requiring isolation and personal struggle.

o **Reality:** Sacrifices can be supported by a community, faith, and relationships. Sharing the burden with others can make sacrifices more manageable and less isolating, fostering a sense of shared purpose and mutual support.

o **Expanded Insight:** Engaging in group activities, such as Bible study or support groups, can provide a network of encouragement and accountability, making the process of sacrifice more enriching and less daunting.

The Role of Sacrifice in Personal Growth

Sacrifice is not merely about giving up something; it's about making room for something better. It's a deliberate choice to prioritize what truly matters, whether that's personal well-being, spiritual growth, or the well-being of others.

1. **Cultivating Resilience:**

   o Sacrifices often require us to endure hardship and discomfort. By navigating these challenges, we build resilience, learning to bounce back from setbacks and maintain our commitment to growth.

2. **Fostering Selflessness:**

   o Sacrifice teaches us to put others first, fostering a sense of selflessness and compassion. This shift in focus from self to others can lead to more meaningful relationships and a deeper sense of purpose.

3. **Encouraging Reflection and Self-Awareness:**

   o The act of sacrificing encourages introspection, prompting us to evaluate what truly matters in our lives. This self-awareness is crucial for making informed decisions that align with our values and goals.

4. **Promoting Spiritual Growth:**

   o Sacrifices often have a spiritual dimension, challenging us to rely on faith and trust in a higher power. This reliance can deepen our spiritual practices and enhance our connection to the divine.

Sacrifice in Daily Life

Sacrifice is not limited to monumental decisions like surgery or life-altering choices. It permeates our daily lives in various subtle forms, each contributing to our overall growth and well-being.

1. **Time Management:**

   o Choosing how to allocate your time involves sacrifices. For instance, dedicating time to a hobby may mean sacrificing leisure time spent on less fulfilling activities.

2. **Financial Decisions:**

   o Financial sacrifices, such as saving money instead of spending on immediate luxuries, can lead to long-term security and opportunities for growth.

3. **Health and Wellness:**

   o Sacrificing unhealthy habits in favor of healthier choices supports both physical and mental well-being.

4. **Relationships:**

   o Investing in meaningful relationships may require sacrificing time spent with acquaintances or engaging in superficial interactions.

Sacrifice and Accountability

Accountability plays a crucial role in maintaining the sacrifices we make. Sharing your goals and commitments with trusted individuals can provide the support and encouragement needed to stay on track.

1. Finding Accountability Partners:

o Partnering with someone who shares similar goals or values can enhance your commitment to sacrifice. They can offer encouragement, share insights, and help you stay focused.

2. Joining Support Groups:

o Support groups, whether in-person or online, provide a community of individuals who understand your journey. They offer a safe space to share challenges and celebrate successes.

3. Engaging with Mentors:

o Mentors can provide guidance, wisdom, and accountability. Their experience and insights can help you navigate sacrifices more effectively.

Balancing Sacrifice and Self-Care

While sacrifice is essential for growth, it's equally important to balance sacrifices with self-care. Neglecting self-care can lead to burnout and diminish the positive outcomes of your sacrifices.

1. **Prioritizing Well-Being:**

   o   Ensure that your sacrifices are contributing to your well-being rather than detracting from it. Assess whether what you're giving up aligns with your values and supports your overall health.

2. **Setting Boundaries:**

   o   Establishing boundaries helps you maintain a healthy balance between sacrifice and self-care. It ensures that your sacrifices are sustainable and do not compromise your well-being.

3. **Listening to Your Body and Mind:**

   o   Pay attention to signs of stress, fatigue, or emotional strain. Adjust your sacrifices as needed to prioritize your health and well-being.

Sacrifice and Faith: A Symbiotic Relationship

Faith and sacrifice are deeply intertwined, each enhancing the other in the journey of personal growth and healing.

1. **Faith as a Motivator:**

   o   Faith often inspires us to make sacrifices, driven by a desire to align our lives with spiritual teachings and values.

2. **Sacrifice as an Act of Faith:**

   o   Making sacrifices can be an expression of faith, demonstrating trust in a higher power and commitment to spiritual growth.

3. **Strengthening Faith through Sacrifice:**

   o   The challenges and rewards of sacrifice can deepen our faith, providing tangible experiences of spiritual principles in action.

Reflection Prompt

*   **What sacrifices have you made in your life for the sake of personal growth or the well-being of others? How did these sacrifices impact your journey?**

Take a moment to reflect on the sacrifices you've made. Consider both significant and subtle sacrifices that have shaped your path. How have these acts of giving influenced your personal development, relationships, and spiritual journey?

Scriptural Insight

"Greater love hath no man than this, that a man lay down his life for his friends." – John 15:13 (KJV)

This scripture encapsulates the essence of selfless sacrifice, highlighting the depth of love and commitment involved in giving something precious for the sake of others. It serves as a reminder that true sacrifice is rooted in love and the desire to see others thrive.

Devotional Reflection

Devotional: The Power of Sacrifice

Scripture: "Greater love hath no man than this, that a man lay down his life for his friends." – John 15:13 (KJV)

Reflection: Jesus's ultimate sacrifice teaches us the profound impact of selflessness. While my own journey involves sacrifices for personal healing and growth, Jesus's sacrifice stands as the supreme example of love and giving. Reflecting on this scripture, consider how your sacrifices, inspired by faith, can nurture both your heart and spirit, even as you honor the unparalleled sacrifice of Christ.

Expanded Reflection: Reflecting on Jesus's sacrifice, I find parallels in my own life's sacrifices, though on a much smaller scale. Just as Jesus gave Himself out of love for humanity, my decision to undergo surgery was driven by a desire to preserve my life and well-being. Both acts required letting go of something valuable—Jesus His life, and me, my veins. Yet, each sacrifice opened the door to renewal and hope. How can I emulate this level of selflessness in my daily interactions? Perhaps by offering support to a friend in need, volunteering my time, or simply being present for those who require companionship and understanding.

Prayer: "Lord, grant me the strength to make the necessary sacrifices for my growth. Help me to trust in Thy plan and find peace in letting go of what hinders my journey. Thank Thee for the ultimate sacrifice of Jesus, which inspires me to live a life of purpose and love."

Conclusion

Understanding sacrifice is the first step toward embracing it as a catalyst for personal growth and healing. By recognizing the value and impact of sacrifices—both personal and spiritual—we can navigate our journeys with greater purpose and resilience, always honoring the ultimate sacrifice made by Jesus Christ.

CHAPTER 2

The Metaphor of Veins and Heart

Symbolism in Personal Experience

The human body is a marvel of intricate systems working in harmony. Among these, the heart and veins play pivotal roles. In my medical journey, the decision to undergo surgery—sacrificing veins from my left leg—became a powerful metaphor for the interconnectedness of our physical, emotional, and spiritual selves. This act represents the sacrifices we make to preserve our core essence, illustrating how actions in one area of life can have profound impacts on others.

In our bodies, veins carry deoxygenated blood back to the heart, ensuring that every part receives the nutrients it needs. In a similar way, the sacrifices we make—whether in time, energy, relationships, or personal comforts—serve to sustain and nourish our heart, the center of our emotions, desires, and spiritual life. Just as a healthy heart depends on a well-functioning network of veins, our overall well-being relies on the deliberate choices we make to let go of what no longer serves us.

Breaking Down the Metaphor

To appreciate the full depth of this metaphor, it helps to consider its key elements:

Veins: Representing Sacrifices

Veins function as essential channels in the body, returning blood to the heart. Here, they symbolize the sacrifices we make in life. These sacrifices—be they relinquishing certain habits, ending draining relationships, or sacrificing personal comforts—are the conduits that facilitate our emotional and spiritual growth. They are the investments we make in our well-being.

Personal Anecdote:

When I chose to undergo surgery and sacrifice veins from my left leg, it was an act of profound dedication. Although the decision came with significant challenges, it reflected a deliberate commitment to preserving the most vital part of me—my heart.

Heart: The Core Essence

The heart is the seat of our emotions, desires, and spiritual energy. It is central to our identity and well-being.

Ensuring its health is crucial—not only physically, but also emotionally and spiritually.

Personal Insight:

For me, safeguarding my heart was paramount. The sacrifices I made were directly tied to keeping my core vibrant and healthy. This idea reinforces that true growth comes from nurturing what is central to our being.

Swollen Legs: Visible Consequences

The swelling in my legs following surgery is a tangible reminder of the sacrifices made. It represents the visible consequences that sometimes accompany our choices, reminding us that sacrifices—though often painful—are a necessary part of our healing process.

Emotional Impact:

The physical swelling served as a daily reminder of the cost of healing, yet it also signified the price paid for the preservation of life and vitality.

Interconnectedness of Body and Soul

This metaphor illustrates that our physical well-being is intertwined with our emotional and spiritual states. Just as veins and heart work together to keep our body functioning, our sacrifices in one area of life can affect our overall health and growth.

Mind-Body Connection

A problem in one area of the body can have ripple effects throughout the entire system. Similarly, emotional or spiritual challenges often manifest physically. For example, during my recovery, the limitations imposed by my swollen leg not only brought physical discomfort but also stirred feelings of frustration and vulnerability. Yet, through faith and a positive outlook, I was able to find emotional resilience that aided my overall healing.

Holistic Approach

Understanding that our well-being depends on nurturing body, mind, and spirit reinforces the need for a holistic approach. Instead of addressing just one area, true healing requires a balanced focus—exercise and nutrition for the body, self-awareness for the mind, and prayer and community for the spirit.

Jesus's Sacrifice: The Ultimate Example

Jesus Christ's sacrifice on the cross is the most profound example of selflessness and love. His willingness to give His life provides a benchmark for the sacrifices we make in our own lives, urging us to view our acts of sacrifice through the lens of faith and redemption.

Scriptural Reference:

"For God so loved the world, that he gave his only begotten Son, that whosoever believeth in him should not perish, but have everlasting life." – **John 3:16 (KJV)**

Jesus's sacrifice invites us to reflect on our own choices—seeing them not as burdens, but as steps toward spiritual renewal. His resurrection symbolizes that from sacrifice comes new life and hope, a message that encourages us to rise above our struggles.

Connecting to Real Life

Daily, we make sacrifices that impact our personal growth. Whether it's investing time in our passions, dedicating energy to meaningful goals, or letting go of relationships that no longer nurture us, these sacrifices shape our journey.

Examples of Daily Sacrifices

- **Time:**
  Choosing to devote time to personal development instead of idle activities.
- **Energy:**
  Allocating energy to pursue meaningful goals, even when it requires stepping outside of our comfort zones.
- **Relationships:**
  Letting go of toxic connections to foster healthier, more supportive bonds.

- **Personal Comforts:**
  Sacrificing small luxuries in order to invest in long-term growth and well-being.

Each of these sacrifices plays a role in our holistic development. They serve as reminders that every choice we make contributes to the balance and health of our overall being.

Conclusion

The metaphor of veins and heart powerfully illustrates that the sacrifices we make—whether physical, emotional, or spiritual—are interconnected and essential for our growth. They enable us to shed what no longer serves us and to nurture the core of our being. By understanding and embracing this interconnectedness, we come to view our sacrifices as investments in our own healing and transformation.

"For God so loved the world, that he gave his only begotten Son, that whosoever believeth in him should not perish, but have everlasting life." – **John 3:16 (KJV)**

May this metaphor inspire you to see your sacrifices not as losses, but as powerful acts that sustain your heart, nurture your soul, and lead you toward a life of balance, purpose, and deep spiritual fulfillment.

CHAPTER 3

Identifying What to Sacrifice

Introduction: The Necessity of Letting Go

Sacrifice begins with the ability to identify what no longer serves us. In my medical journey, the decision to sacrifice veins from my leg was a clear and necessary step for survival. Similarly, in our personal lives, recognizing what to let go of is crucial for growth and healing.

Identifying what to sacrifice requires deep self-awareness and honesty. It involves examining various aspects of our lives and determining which elements hinder our progress, well-being, or spiritual growth. This process is not about merely giving up; it's about making room for what truly matters and aligns with our values and purpose.

As Jesus taught in Matthew 16:24 (KJV), *"Then said Jesus unto his disciples, If any man will come after me, let him deny himself, and take up his cross, and follow me."* This verse encapsulates the essence of sacrifice—denying oneself to embrace a higher purpose. Understanding what to sacrifice

---

is the first step toward aligning our lives with divine will and achieving meaningful growth.

Section 1: Self-Assessment Tools

To effectively identify what to sacrifice, utilizing self-assessment tools can provide clarity and direction. These tools help us evaluate different areas of our lives, rate our satisfaction, and align our actions with our core values.

Exercise: Life Inventory

Instructions:

1. **List Different Areas of Your Life:**

    o   Relationships
    o   Career
    o   Health
    o   Spirituality
    o   Personal Growth
    o   Leisure and Hobbies
    o   Financial Stability

2. **Rate Your Satisfaction:**

    o   On a scale of 1-10, rate your satisfaction in each area.

3. **Identify Low-Rated Areas:**

    o   Highlight the areas with the lowest ratings as potential candidates for sacrifice.

Reflection:

- *"Which areas of your life are causing you the most stress or dissatisfaction? What might happen if you reduced your involvement or let go of certain aspects in these areas?"*

Expanded Insight:

Conducting a Life Inventory provides a comprehensive overview of where you currently stand in various aspects of your life. It allows you to pinpoint areas that may be draining your energy or impeding your growth. By identifying these low-rated areas, you can prioritize which aspects to address first, ensuring that your sacrifices lead to meaningful and positive change.

Personal Example: Reflecting on my own Life Inventory, I noticed that my career was highly stressful and left me with little time for personal relationships or spiritual practices. This imbalance was contributing to feelings of burnout and spiritual disconnection. Recognizing this, I decided to make sacrifices in my work life—such as delegating tasks and setting stricter boundaries—to create space for healing and personal growth.

Exercise: Values Assessment

Instructions:

1. Identify Your Core Values:

- o List 5-10 core values (e.g., honesty, compassion, growth, faith, resilience).

2. **Align Areas of Your Life with Values:**

   o   For each area identified in the Life Inventory, assess how well it aligns with your core values.

3. **Identify Conflicting Areas:**

   o   Determine which areas are currently compromising your core values and may require sacrifice.

Reflection:

   •   *"How do the sacrifices you make align with your core values? Are there areas where your actions are not in harmony with what you truly value?"*

Expanded Insight:

A Values Assessment helps you understand what is most important to you and ensures that your sacrifices are purposeful and aligned with your true self. It prevents you from making sacrifices out of habit or societal pressure, ensuring that each sacrifice contributes to your authentic growth and fulfillment.

Personal Example: My core values include health, faith, and family. During my Life Inventory, I realized that my career was taking precedence over these values, leading to neglect in my personal relationships and spiritual practices. By aligning my sacrifices with my core values, I decided to prioritize my health and family over career advancement, allowing me to cultivate a more balanced and fulfilling life.

Section 2: Prioritizing Sacrifices

Once you've identified potential areas for sacrifice, the next step is to prioritize them based on their impact on your overall well-being and alignment with your values.

Identifying Non-Essential Elements

Just as my left leg was a source of life for my heart, certain aspects of our lives, though valuable, may need to be relinquished to foster growth. Reflecting on Jesus's sacrifice, we see the profound impact of letting go for a higher purpose.

Guiding Questions:

- What elements of your life feel burdensome or limiting?
- Which areas provide the least fulfillment or value?
- How does letting go of these elements align with your personal and spiritual goals?

Personal Insight: In my journey, I realized that excessive commitment to work was leaving me with little time for family and spiritual practices. This imbalance was detrimental to my overall well-being. By identifying work-related stress as a non-essential element that was hindering my growth, I was able to make conscious sacrifices to restore balance.

Impact Analysis

Evaluating the potential impact of each sacrifice helps you understand the consequences and benefits of letting go.

This analysis ensures that your sacrifices lead to positive outcomes and support your growth.

Steps:

1. **List Potential Sacrifices:**

   o From the identified non-essential elements, list potential sacrifices.

2. **Assess Impact:**

   o For each potential sacrifice, assess the short-term and long-term impact on your life.

3. **Consider Spiritual Growth:**

   o How will this sacrifice contribute to your spiritual and personal growth?

Expanded Insight:

Impact Analysis allows you to foresee the outcomes of your sacrifices, both positive and negative. It helps in making informed decisions, ensuring that each sacrifice aligns with your long-term goals and values.

Personal Example: Sacrificing time spent on social media was a significant decision. In the short term, it meant reducing my online presence and staying away from certain platforms. However, in the long term, it led to increased productivity, improved mental health, and more time for meaningful activities like reading and prayer, which contributed to my spiritual growth.

Decision-Making Framework

Introducing a structured framework can aid in prioritizing sacrifices, ensuring that your decisions are thoughtful and aligned with your values and faith.

Framework: Pros and Cons with Spiritual Alignment

1. **List Pros and Cons:**

   o For each potential sacrifice, list the benefits and drawbacks.

2. **Evaluate Alignment with Values:**

   o How well does this sacrifice align with your core values and faith?

3. **Make a Decision:**

   o Prioritize sacrifices that have high benefits, align closely with your values, and support your spiritual growth.

Personal Insight: Using this framework, I evaluated the pros and cons of reducing my work hours. The pros included more time for family and spiritual activities, while the cons involved potential financial strain. However, the alignment with my core values of family and faith outweighed the financial concerns, leading me to make the necessary adjustments.

Section 3: Case Studies and Examples

Real-life and fictional examples can provide tangible illustrations of how identifying and prioritizing sacrifices lead to personal growth and healing.

Real-Life Example: Sarah's Journey

Sarah's Journey:

Sarah was working in a high-stress corporate job that left her feeling unfulfilled and constantly anxious. Inspired by her faith and desire for a more meaningful life, she chose to leave her job to pursue her passion for teaching. This sacrifice led to increased happiness, fulfillment, and a deeper connection with her community, demonstrating the positive impact of aligning sacrifices with personal values and spiritual beliefs.

Expanded Insight:

Sarah's decision to leave her corporate job was not just about changing careers; it was about realigning her life with her core values of service, education, and community. This shift required courage and a willingness to face uncertainty, but the rewards were profound. Her story illustrates how prioritizing what truly matters can lead to a more satisfying and purpose-driven life.

Fictional Example: John's Transformation

John's Transformation:

John was in a toxic relationship that drained his emotional energy and hindered his personal growth. Recognizing the need for change, he decided to end the relationship, prioritizing his mental and spiritual health. This decision allowed him to focus on his faith, build healthier relationships, and pursue his goals with renewed vigor, illustrating the importance of letting go of negative influences to embrace positive transformation.

Expanded Insight:

John's journey highlights the significance of emotional sacrifices in fostering personal growth. By ending a draining relationship, he made space for positive influences and healthier connections, both emotionally and spiritually. His transformation underscores the importance of making tough decisions to protect and nurture one's well-being.

Section 4: Action Steps

Providing actionable steps helps readers implement the concepts discussed in the chapter, ensuring that they can apply these lessons to their own lives.

Worksheet: What Can I Let Go Of?

Instructions:

1. **List Potential Sacrifices:**

   o Based on your Life Inventory and Values Assessment, list the elements you can consider sacrificing.

2. **Assess Each Sacrifice:**

   o Use the Pros and Cons with Spiritual Alignment framework to evaluate each potential sacrifice.

3. **Prioritize:**

   o Rank your sacrifices based on their impact and alignment with your values and faith.

Purpose: This worksheet helps you systematically evaluate and prioritize your sacrifices, ensuring that your decisions are aligned with your personal and spiritual goals.

Guided Reflection:

- *"What do I hold onto that hinders my growth?"*
- *"How would my life improve if I let go of this?"*
- *"In what ways can my faith guide me in making these sacrifices?"*

Expanded Insight:

Reflecting on these questions encourages deep introspection, allowing you to identify and release the elements that impede your growth. It also reinforces the role of faith in guiding your decisions, ensuring that your sacrifices are purposeful and aligned with your spiritual journey.

Scriptural Insight

"And Jesus said unto him, If any man will come after me, let him deny himself, and take up his cross, and follow me." – Matthew 16:24 (KJV)

This scripture emphasizes the importance of self-denial and sacrifice in following Christ. It underscores the necessity of letting go of personal desires and comforts to pursue a higher spiritual calling, aligning perfectly with the chapter's theme of identifying and prioritizing sacrifices for personal and spiritual growth.

Devotional Reflection

Devotional: Embracing Necessary Sacrifices

Scripture: "And Jesus said unto him, If any man will come after me, let him deny himself, and take up his cross, and follow me." – Matthew 16:24 (KJV)

Reflection: Following Jesus requires a commitment to sacrifice and self-denial. This journey is not about losing oneself but about gaining a deeper connection with the divine purpose. Reflecting on this scripture, consider how your sacrifices are an act of faith, demonstrating your willingness to align your life with God's will.

Expanded Reflection: Jesus's call to deny oneself and take up the cross is a profound invitation to embrace sacrifice for a higher purpose. In my journey, identifying what to sacrifice was both a challenge and a blessing. It required me to confront my attachments and prioritize what truly mattered—health, faith, and meaningful relationships. Each sacrifice was an act of trust in God's plan, reinforcing my commitment to personal and spiritual growth. How can I embody this level of dedication in my daily life? Perhaps by setting aside time for prayer, letting go of negative thoughts, or dedicating myself to acts of service and compassion.

Prayer: "Lord, grant me the courage to identify and embrace the sacrifices necessary for my growth. Help me to trust in Your plan and to let go of what hinders my journey. May my sacrifices be a testament to my faith and commitment to following You."

Conclusion

Identifying what to sacrifice is a brave and necessary step toward healing. By using self-assessment tools and reflecting on personal and spiritual values, you can make intentional sacrifices that lead to profound personal and spiritual growth.

Sacrifice, when understood and implemented thoughtfully, becomes a powerful tool for transformation. It allows us to shed what no longer serves us, embrace what truly matters, and nurture the heart that lies at the center of our being. Through this chapter, we have explored the importance of self-awareness, the alignment of sacrifices with core values, and the practical steps to prioritize and implement these sacrifices in our lives.

Embracing necessary sacrifices is not about deprivation but about making conscious choices that align with our highest values and spiritual commitments. It is about trusting in a higher purpose and recognizing that through sacrifice, we create space for growth, renewal, and deeper connection with the divine.

CHAPTER 4

The Process of Healing

Introduction: The Journey Begins

Healing is a multifaceted process that encompasses physical recovery, emotional resilience, and spiritual renewal. My journey through surgery and recovery was not just about restoring my heart but also about embracing the transformations that come with sacrifice. Healing is not linear; it involves navigating through various stages, each presenting its own set of challenges and opportunities for growth. Understanding these stages and embracing vulnerability are essential components of a successful healing journey.

In Psalm 147:3, it is written, *"He healeth the broken in heart, and bindeth up their wounds."* This scripture encapsulates the essence of healing—mending what is broken and restoring wholeness. As we embark on the process of healing, it is crucial to recognize that it is a divine journey supported by faith, personal effort, and the grace of God.

Section 1: Stages of Healing

Healing can be broken down into distinct stages, each marking a significant phase in the recovery process. Recognizing and understanding these stages can provide clarity and help manage expectations during your healing journey.

Denial

Initially, denial is a common reaction to a life-altering event or diagnosis. This stage serves as a protective mechanism, allowing us to cope with overwhelming emotions and information.

When I first received my diagnosis, denial was my immediate response. The thought of undergoing surgery and sacrificing part of my leg seemed almost surreal. I found myself avoiding discussions about the procedure, hoping that the problem would somehow resolve itself without intervention. This stage was marked by fear and resistance, where the severity of my situation seemed almost insurmountable.

Isaiah 53:5 states, *"But he was wounded for our transgressions, he was bruised for our iniquities: the chastisement of our peace was upon him; and with his stripes we are healed."* This scripture reflects the initial resistance and the deep-seated wounds that one must confront to begin the healing process.

Reflection Prompt: Reflect on a time when you experienced denial. How did this stage affect your ability to seek help or accept necessary changes?

Practical Exercise: Acknowledgment Journal

- **Daily Entry:** Write about your feelings and thoughts regarding your current situation.
- **Identify Emotions:** Acknowledge emotions such as fear, anger, or confusion without judgment.
- **Acceptance Statements:** End each entry with a statement of acceptance or a step towards understanding your situation.

This exercise helps in recognizing and validating your emotions, facilitating a gradual transition from denial to acceptance.

Acceptance

Gradually, acceptance sets in as we come to terms with the reality of our situation. Embracing this truth is the first step toward genuine healing. It involves acknowledging the necessity of change and trusting in the process that will lead to recovery.

Acceptance did not mean I was devoid of fear or anxiety. Instead, it signified my acknowledgment of these emotions and my decision to face them head-on. I began to see the surgery not as an end but as an opportunity for renewal and a healthier life.

John 14:27 offers reassurance: *"Peace I leave with you, my peace I give unto you: not as the world giveth, give I unto you. Let not your heart be troubled, neither let it be afraid."* This scripture provides comfort and reinforces the importance of acceptance in the healing journey.

Reflection Prompt: How did acceptance change your perspective on your healing process? What benefits did you experience by embracing acceptance?

Practical Exercise: Acceptance Affirmations

- **Create Affirmations:** Write down positive affirmations that reinforce acceptance (e.g., "I accept the reality of my situation and trust in the healing process.").
- **Daily Practice:** Repeat these affirmations each morning and evening.
- **Visualization:** As you recite each affirmation, visualize yourself embracing acceptance and moving forward with confidence.

Affirmations help in solidifying the mindset of acceptance, promoting a positive and proactive approach to healing.

Transformation

Post-recovery, a profound transformation occurs—not just physically healed but emotionally and spiritually renewed. This transformation mirrors the renewal symbolized by Jesus's resurrection, offering hope and the assurance of new beginnings.

The transformation I experienced was multifaceted. Physically, my heart was healthier, but emotionally and spiritually, I felt a deeper connection to my faith and a greater appreciation for life. This renewed sense of purpose and resilience continues to guide me, encouraging me to embrace future challenges with confidence and grace.

2 Corinthians 5:17 beautifully encapsulates the essence of transformation: *"Therefore if any man be in Christ, he is a new creature: old things are passed away; behold, all things are become new."* This scripture highlights the rebirth and renewal that comes from embracing faith and healing.

Reflection Prompt: In what ways have you transformed emotionally and spiritually through your healing journey? How has this transformation impacted your daily life?

Practical Exercise: Transformation Timeline

- **Draw a Timeline:** Create a timeline starting from the beginning of your healing journey to the present.
- **Mark Milestones:** Identify key moments of transformation, such as overcoming fears, achieving milestones, or deepening your faith.
- **Reflect:** Write a brief reflection on how each milestone contributed to your overall transformation.

This exercise allows you to visualize and acknowledge the progress and growth achieved through your healing journey.

Section 2: Embracing Vulnerability

Healing requires us to embrace vulnerability, allowing ourselves to be open to emotions, support, and growth.

The Power of Openness

Being open and vulnerable during the healing process allows for deep emotional connections and authentic healing.

Vulnerability is not a sign of weakness but a strength that fosters genuine connections and emotional restoration.

During my recovery, I found solace in sharing my fears and struggles with loved ones. This openness not only provided emotional relief but also strengthened my bonds with family and friends. Their support and understanding were instrumental in my healing, proving that vulnerability can lead to profound connection and support.

Psalm 91:2 offers assurance: *"I will say of the LORD, He is my refuge and my fortress: my God; in him will I trust."* This scripture emphasizes trust and openness in seeking refuge and support, highlighting the strength found in vulnerability.

Reflection Prompt: How has embracing vulnerability facilitated your healing process? What benefits have you experienced from being open with others?

Practical Exercise: Vulnerability Sharing Circle

- **Identify Trusted Individuals:** Choose a few trusted friends or family members with whom you feel safe sharing your feelings.
- **Schedule a Meeting:** Arrange a time to meet and share your experiences and emotions.
- **Engage in Active Listening:** Encourage open dialogue where everyone listens without judgment.
- **Express Gratitude:** Thank each participant for their support and understanding.

This exercise fosters emotional connections and provides a safe space for sharing and healing through vulnerability.

Faith as a Support

Turning to prayer and scripture provides comfort and strength, helping navigate the uncertainties of recovery. Faith becomes a beacon of hope, guiding us through moments of doubt and fear.

My faith was a cornerstone of my healing journey. Daily prayers and scripture readings provided me with peace and clarity, helping me stay focused on the positive aspects of my recovery. The belief in a higher purpose and divine plan gave me the courage to endure the sacrifices and challenges I faced.

Proverbs 3:5 reinforces this reliance: *"Trust in the LORD with all thine heart; and lean not unto thine own understanding."* This scripture encourages trust in God, emphasizing the importance of faith over personal understanding during the healing process.

Reflection Prompt: In what ways has your faith supported you during your healing journey? How can you incorporate spiritual counseling into your recovery process?

Practical Exercise: Daily Prayer and Meditation

- **Set a Routine:** Dedicate specific times each day for prayer and meditation.
- **Focus on Gratitude:** Begin each session by expressing gratitude for the progress made and the support received.
- **Seek Guidance:** Use prayers to seek strength, clarity, and guidance for the challenges ahead.
- **Reflect:** After each session, jot down any insights or feelings that arose during prayer and meditation.

This practice strengthens your spiritual connection and provides continual support and guidance throughout your healing journey.

Section 3: Mind-Body Connection

Understanding the mind-body connection is crucial for a holistic approach to healing. Our physical health is deeply intertwined with our emotional and spiritual well-being.

Physical Health and Emotional Well-Being

Healing the heart had a ripple effect on my emotional state. As my physical health improved, so did my sense of hope and resilience. The mind-body connection is undeniable; improving one aspect of our well-being often enhances others.

As my heart healed, I noticed a significant improvement in my mood and outlook on life. The physical relief translated into emotional stability, allowing me to engage more fully with my faith and personal relationships. This interconnectedness highlighted the importance of addressing both physical and emotional aspects of healing.

Psalm 147:3 underscores the holistic nature of healing: *"He healeth the broken in heart, and bindeth up their wounds."* This scripture addresses both physical and emotional wounds, emphasizing the need for comprehensive healing.

Reflection Prompt: How has improving your physical health impacted your emotional and spiritual well-being? What changes have you noticed in your overall outlook on life?

Practical Exercise: Integrated Health Plan

- **Assess Current Health:** Evaluate your physical, emotional, and spiritual health.
- **Set Goals:** Establish specific goals for each area (e.g., physical exercise, emotional resilience practices, spiritual growth activities).
- **Create a Schedule:** Develop a balanced schedule that incorporates activities addressing all three aspects.
- **Monitor Progress:** Regularly review and adjust your plan to ensure balanced progress.

This exercise promotes a balanced approach to health, recognizing the interdependence of physical, emotional, and spiritual well-being.

Spiritual Nourishment

Just as veins sustain the heart, spiritual practices nourish the soul, fostering a holistic approach to healing. Engaging in prayer, meditation, and spiritual reflection enriches the healing process, providing deeper insights and a sense of purpose.

Incorporating spiritual practices into my daily routine was transformative. Prayer and meditation not only provided comfort but also guided me in making meaningful sacrifices. These practices deepened my understanding of sacrifice as an act of faith and love, reinforcing my commitment to personal and spiritual growth.

Jeremiah 29:11 offers assurance of divine plans: *"For I know the thoughts that I think toward you, saith the LORD, thoughts of peace, and not of evil, to give you an expected end."*

This scripture provides assurance of God's benevolent plans, reinforcing the hope and purpose that faith brings to the healing journey.

Reflection Prompt: What spiritual practices have you found most nourishing during your healing journey? How can you integrate these practices more deeply into your daily life?

Practical Exercise: Spiritual Growth Plan

- **Identify Practices:** List spiritual practices that resonate with you (e.g., prayer, scripture study, meditation).
- **Set Intentions:** Define specific intentions for each practice (e.g., deepen understanding, seek guidance, find peace).
- **Create a Routine:** Schedule regular times for each spiritual practice.
- **Reflect and Adjust:** Periodically reflect on the impact of these practices and make adjustments as needed.

This exercise fosters consistent spiritual growth, providing a structured approach to nurturing your soul and supporting overall healing.

Section 4: Expert Insights

Gaining insights from medical and spiritual experts can enhance our understanding of the healing process and provide valuable strategies for overcoming challenges.

Medical Perspectives

Medical professionals emphasize the importance of a holistic approach to healing, addressing not just the physical ailment but also the emotional and psychological aspects. Integrative medicine, which combines traditional treatments with complementary therapies, plays a crucial role in comprehensive healing.

Learning about integrative medicine reinforced the importance of addressing all aspects of my being during the healing process. It encouraged me to seek out therapies that supported my emotional and spiritual health, complementing the medical treatments I was receiving.

Isaiah 58:11 offers comfort and guidance: *"And the LORD shall guide thee continually, and satisfy thy soul in drought, and make fat thy bones: and thou shalt be like a watered garden, and like a spring of water, whose waters fail not."* This scripture reflects the comprehensive guidance and sustenance that God provides, aligning with the holistic approach advocated by medical professionals.

Expert Quote: *"True healing goes beyond the physical symptoms. It involves addressing the emotional and spiritual dimensions to achieve lasting wellness."* – Dr. Emily Thompson, Integrative Medicine Specialist

Reflection Prompt: How can integrating medical and spiritual practices enhance your healing process? What steps can you take to adopt a more holistic approach to your health?

Practical Exercise: Holistic Health Integration

- **Identify Complementary Therapies:** Research and select complementary therapies that align with your needs (e.g., acupuncture, massage, mindfulness meditation).

- **Consult Professionals:** Speak with healthcare providers and spiritual advisors to create an integrated healing plan.
- **Implement Practices:** Incorporate these therapies into your routine alongside traditional medical treatments.
- **Evaluate Effectiveness:** Regularly assess the impact of these integrated practices on your overall well-being.

This exercise encourages a comprehensive approach to health, combining medical treatments with complementary therapies to support holistic healing.

Spiritual Guidance

Spiritual leaders advocate for the integration of faith and healing, recognizing that spiritual well-being significantly impacts overall health. Practices such as prayer, meditation, and community support are essential components of a spiritual healing journey.

Connecting with a spiritual counselor helped me navigate the emotional complexities of my healing journey. Their guidance provided me with strategies to integrate faith into my daily life, fostering a deeper sense of purpose and strength.

James 4:8 emphasizes the importance of drawing near to God: *"Draw near to God, and he will draw near to you."* This scripture highlights the reciprocal relationship between seeking God and receiving His presence, reinforcing the importance of spiritual guidance in the healing process.

Expert Quote: *"Faith provides a foundation for resilience and hope, essential elements in the healing journey."* – Reverend Mark Johnson, Spiritual Counselor

Reflection Prompt: In what ways can seeking spiritual guidance support your healing journey? How can you incorporate spiritual counseling into your recovery process?

Practical Exercise: Engage with a Spiritual Counselor

- **Identify a Counselor:** Find a trusted spiritual counselor or advisor who aligns with your faith and values.
- **Schedule Sessions:** Arrange regular meetings to discuss your healing journey and seek guidance.
- **Set Goals:** Define specific spiritual goals you wish to achieve through counseling.
- **Implement Advice:** Apply the insights and strategies provided by your counselor to your daily life.

This exercise facilitates deeper spiritual understanding and support, enhancing emotional and spiritual resilience during the healing process.

Section 5: Inspirational Stories

Inspirational stories of individuals who have overcome similar challenges can provide hope and motivation, illustrating the effectiveness of the strategies discussed.

Personal Transformation

My own transformation post-surgery was a testament to the power of resilience and faith. Each day brought new challenges, but also new strengths and insights, culminating in a renewed heart and spirit.

The transformation I experienced was multifaceted. Physically, my heart was healthier, but emotionally and spiritually, I felt a deeper connection to my faith and a greater appreciation for life. This renewed sense of purpose and resilience continues to guide me, encouraging me to embrace future challenges with confidence and grace.

Romans 8:28 encapsulates the belief that every aspect of our journey serves a greater purpose: *"And we know that all things work together for good to them that love God, to them who are the called according to his purpose."* This scripture reinforces the idea that sacrifices and challenges contribute to our overall good and spiritual growth.

Reflection Prompt: How has your personal journey of healing and sacrifice transformed you emotionally and spiritually? What lessons have you learned that can inspire others?

Practical Exercise: Share Your Story

- **Write Your Experience:** Document your healing journey, highlighting key sacrifices, challenges, and transformations.
- **Identify Lessons Learned:** Reflect on the insights and lessons gained through your experience.
- **Share with Others:** Consider sharing your story with a support group, blog, or community to inspire and encourage others.

- **Seek Feedback:** Engage with your audience to provide support and receive encouragement in return.

Sharing your story fosters connection, provides inspiration to others, and reinforces your own healing and transformation.

Faith-Based Renewal

Maria, a member of my faith community, shared her story of overcoming a severe illness through unwavering faith and community support. Her journey mirrored my own, highlighting the transformative power of faith in the healing process.

Maria's story illustrates how faith and community support can be instrumental in overcoming personal struggles. Her reliance on prayer, scripture, and the support of her faith community provided her with the strength and resilience needed to endure her illness. This narrative underscores the importance of integrating faith into the healing process and leveraging community support for emotional and spiritual sustenance.

Jeremiah 29:11 offers assurance of divine plans: *"For I know the thoughts that I think toward you, saith the LORD, thoughts of peace, and not of evil, to give you an expected end."* This scripture provides assurance of God's benevolent plans, reinforcing the hope and purpose that faith brings to the healing journey.

Reflection Prompt: How have stories of faith-based renewal inspired you in your healing process? What aspects of these stories resonate most with your own experiences?

Practical Exercise: Engage with Faith Community Stories

- **Attend Community Events:** Participate in faith-based gatherings where stories of healing and renewal are shared.
- **Listen Actively:** Pay attention to the experiences and insights of others, seeking lessons and inspiration.
- **Reflect and Apply:** Consider how the stories align with your own journey and apply relevant lessons to your healing process.
- **Share Your Insights:** Discuss the stories with others to foster mutual understanding and support.

Engaging with stories of faith-based renewal provides encouragement, reinforces belief in divine support, and offers practical insights for your own healing journey.

Reflection Prompt

- **Reflect on the stages of your own healing journey. How have you moved through denial, acceptance, and transformation?**
- **In what ways has your faith supported your healing process?**

Reflecting on these questions encourages you to trace your own healing journey, identifying the phases you've experienced and the role faith has played in each stage. This reflection can provide clarity, foster gratitude, and highlight areas for continued growth.

Scriptural Insight

"The Lord is nigh unto them that are of a broken heart; and saveth such as be of a contrite spirit." – Psalm 34:18 (KJV)

This scripture underscores the comforting presence of God during our most challenging times, offering solace and strength as we navigate the healing process.

Devotional Reflection

Devotional: Embracing the Healing Journey

Scripture: "The Lord is nigh unto them that are of a broken heart; and saveth such as be of a contrite spirit." – Psalm 34:18 (KJV)

Reflection: Healing is not just a physical process but a spiritual journey that involves the restoration of the heart, both emotionally and spiritually. Psalm 34:18 offers profound comfort, reminding us that God is close to those who are brokenhearted and saves those who are crushed in spirit. This assurance allows us to embrace vulnerability, seek divine support, and trust in God's plan for our healing.

In moments of despair and brokenness, turning to God provides a sanctuary of peace and strength. My own healing journey was fraught with challenges that tested my faith and resilience. However, the knowledge that God is near offered me solace and the courage to persevere. Embracing my brokenness allowed me to receive God's healing touch, fostering a deeper connection with Him and a renewed sense of purpose. How can I open my heart to God's presence during times of struggle? By seeking His guidance through prayer, meditating on scripture, and surrounding myself with a supportive faith community, I can navigate the healing process with unwavering faith and hope.

Prayer: "Lord, thank You for being close to me in my times of need. Help me to embrace my vulnerabilities and seek Your guidance in my healing journey. Strengthen my spirit and renew my heart, that I may find peace and restoration through Your love and grace."

Practical Application

- **Exercise: Healing Timeline**

   Instructions:

   1. **Create a Timeline:** Draw a timeline of your healing journey, marking significant milestones such as diagnosis, surgery, recovery stages, and moments of personal growth.
   2. **Reflect on Each Milestone:** Write a brief reflection on what you learned and how each stage contributed to your overall healing.
   3. **Identify Patterns:** Look for patterns or recurring themes that have emerged throughout your journey.

- **Purpose:** This exercise helps you visualize your healing process, recognize your progress, and identify areas where further growth is needed.

- **Exercise: Faith Integration**

Instructions:

1. **List Spiritual Practices:** Identify spiritual practices that have supported your healing (e.g., prayer, meditation, scripture reading).
2. **Commit to Regular Practice:** Schedule time each day or week to engage in these practices.
3. **Reflect on Impact:** After each practice session, jot down how it has influenced your healing and personal growth.

- **Purpose:** Integrating faith-based practices into your daily routine reinforces your spiritual connection and supports continuous healing.

These practical exercises ensure that the lessons from the chapter are not only understood but also actively applied. By mapping your healing timeline and integrating faith-based practices, you create a structured approach to your healing journey, fostering both personal and spiritual development.

Conclusion

Healing is a comprehensive journey that requires addressing physical, emotional, and spiritual dimensions. By embracing vulnerability, fostering a strong mind-body connection, and seeking both medical and spiritual support, you can navigate the healing process with grace and resilience.

Healing is not merely about restoring what was lost but about transforming and renewing oneself. It involves shedding old burdens, embracing new strengths, and cultivating a deeper connection with faith and community. As you progress through your healing journey, remember that each step, each sacrifice, and each moment of vulnerability contributes to your overall well-being and spiritual growth.

In the words of Jeremiah 30:17 (KJV), *"For I will restore health unto thee, and I will heal thee of thy wounds, saith the LORD."* This promise serves as a beacon of hope and assurance that through faith, resilience, and intentional actions, healing and renewal are attainable.

CHAPTER 5

―

Overcoming Challenges and Resistance

Introduction: Embracing the Struggle

The journey of healing and personal growth is often fraught with challenges and resistance. These obstacles can manifest in various forms—physical pain, emotional turmoil, mental blocks, or spiritual doubts. Overcoming these hurdles is essential for progressing towards a more fulfilled and resilient self. Just as iron sharpens iron, the difficulties we encounter can refine our character, deepen our faith, and strengthen our resolve.

In Philippians 4:13 (KJV), the Apostle Paul declares, *"I can do all things through Christ which strengtheneth me."* This powerful affirmation underscores the importance of relying on divine strength when facing adversities. Embracing challenges as opportunities for growth, rather than insurmountable barriers, transforms our approach to healing and sacrifice.

Section 1: Understanding the Nature of Resistance

Resistance is a natural part of any significant change or healing process. It often arises from fear, uncertainty, or attachment to the familiar. Understanding the root causes of resistance can empower us to address and overcome it effectively.

Identifying Sources of Resistance

Resistance can stem from various sources, including:

1. **Fear of the Unknown:** The uncertainty that comes with change can be intimidating. We fear losing control or not knowing what lies ahead.
2. **Comfort Zones:** Familiar routines and environments provide a sense of security. Stepping out of these zones requires courage and effort.
3. **Past Experiences:** Negative past experiences can create apprehensions about future endeavors, leading to hesitation or avoidance.
4. **Self-Doubt:** Lack of confidence in our abilities can hinder progress, making us question whether we can overcome the challenges we face.
5. **External Influences:** Societal expectations, peer pressure, or unsupportive relationships can contribute to internal resistance.

Personal Insight: Reflecting on my own journey, I recognized that fear of the unknown was a significant barrier. The thought of undergoing surgery and the subsequent recovery process was daunting. However, acknowledging this fear was the first step toward overcoming it.

Scriptural Insight

James 1:2-4 (KJV) advises, *"My brethren, count it all joy when ye fall into divers temptations; Knowing this, that the trying of your faith worketh patience. But let patience have her perfect work, that ye may be perfect and entire, wanting nothing."* This passage highlights the value of embracing challenges with a positive outlook, viewing them as opportunities to develop patience and resilience.

Reflection Prompt: What fears or uncertainties are holding you back from fully embracing your healing journey? How can acknowledging these fears help you overcome them?

Section 2: Strategies for Overcoming Challenges

Developing effective strategies to navigate challenges is crucial for maintaining momentum in your healing and growth journey. These strategies can be practical, emotional, and spiritual, providing a comprehensive approach to overcoming resistance.

1. Cultivating a Positive Mindset

A positive mindset transforms how we perceive and respond to challenges. It fosters resilience, enabling us to bounce back from setbacks and maintain motivation.

Personal Insight: Adopting a positive outlook during my recovery made a significant difference. Instead of dwelling on the pain and limitations, I focused on the progress I was making and the opportunities for personal growth that arose from my sacrifices.

Scriptural Insight: Romans 12:12 (KJV) states, *"Rejoicing in hope; patient in tribulation; continuing instant in prayer."* This verse emphasizes the importance of maintaining hope, patience, and a steadfast prayer life in the face of challenges.

Practical Exercise: Gratitude Journal

- **Instructions:**

  1. **Daily Entries:** Each day, write down three things you are grateful for.
  2. **Reflect on Positives:** Focus on positive aspects of your healing journey, no matter how small.
  3. **Review Regularly:** At the end of each week, review your entries to reinforce a positive mindset.

Purpose: This exercise shifts your focus from what is going wrong to what is going right, fostering a sense of gratitude and positivity.

2. Building Emotional Resilience

Emotional resilience is the ability to adapt to stressful situations and recover from adversity. It involves managing emotions effectively and maintaining a balanced perspective.

Personal Insight: Developing emotional resilience allowed me to navigate the emotional ups and downs of recovery. Techniques such as deep breathing, mindfulness, and seeking support from loved ones were instrumental in maintaining emotional balance.

Scriptural Insight: Psalm 34:18 (KJV) offers comfort: *"The LORD is nigh unto them that are of a broken heart; and saveth such as be of a contrite spirit."* This verse reassures us that God is close to those who are struggling emotionally, providing strength and solace.

Practical Exercise: Mindfulness Meditation

- **Instructions:**

    4. **Set Aside Time:** Dedicate 10-15 minutes each day for mindfulness meditation.
    5. **Focus on Breathing:** Concentrate on your breath, observing each inhale and exhale.
    6. **Observe Thoughts:** Acknowledge any thoughts or emotions that arise without judgment.
    7. **Return to Breath:** Gently bring your focus back to your breathing whenever your mind wanders.

Purpose: Mindfulness meditation enhances emotional resilience by promoting calmness, reducing stress, and improving emotional regulation.

3. Seeking Support Systems

Having a robust support system is essential for overcoming challenges. Support can come from family, friends, faith communities, or professional counselors.

Personal Insight: Leaning on my support system during recovery provided me with encouragement, practical assistance, and emotional comfort. Their unwavering support played a pivotal role in my healing process.

Scriptural Insight: Ecclesiastes 4:9-10 (KJV) highlights the value of companionship: *"Two are better than one; because they have a good reward for their labour. For if they fall, the one will lift up his fellow: but woe to him that is alone when he falleth; for he hath not another to help him up."* This passage underscores the importance of mutual support in overcoming difficulties.

Practical Exercise: Support Network Map

- **Instructions:**

    8. **Identify Supporters:** List individuals who provide emotional, practical, or spiritual support.
    9. **Categorize Support:** Determine the type of support each person offers (e.g., emotional, financial, spiritual).
    10. **Enhance Connections:** Identify ways to strengthen these relationships and seek additional support if needed.

Purpose: Mapping your support network helps you recognize available resources and ensures you have the necessary support to navigate challenges.

4. Strengthening Spiritual Practices

Spiritual practices provide a foundation of strength and guidance during difficult times. They offer a sense of purpose, hope, and connection to a higher power.

Personal Insight: Engaging in regular prayer and scripture study fortified my spirit, providing clarity and peace amidst the turmoil of recovery. These practices reinforced my faith and offered a steady source of strength.

Scriptural Insight: Isaiah 40:31 (KJV) promises, *"But they that wait upon the LORD shall renew their strength; they shall mount up with wings as eagles; they shall run, and not be weary; and they shall walk, and not faint."* This scripture emphasizes the renewal of strength that comes from trusting in the Lord.

Practical Exercise: Daily Scripture Reflection

- **Instructions:**

    11. **Choose a Scripture:** Select a verse each day that resonates with your current challenges.
    12. **Reflect:** Spend time meditating on the meaning of the verse and how it applies to your situation.
    13. **Journal Insights:** Write down any insights or feelings that arise during your reflection.
    14. **Apply Lessons:** Identify practical ways to incorporate the teachings of the scripture into your daily life.

Purpose: Daily scripture reflection deepens your spiritual connection, providing wisdom and encouragement to overcome challenges.

Section 3: Practical Tools for Overcoming Resistance

Implementing practical tools and techniques can significantly enhance your ability to overcome resistance and navigate challenges effectively.

1. Time Management Techniques

Effective time management helps you prioritize tasks, reduce stress, and create space for healing and personal growth.

Personal Insight: Organizing my daily schedule allowed me to allocate dedicated time for healing activities, spiritual practices, and personal reflections. This structure prevented overwhelm and ensured balanced progress.

Scriptural Insight: Colossians 3:23 (KJV) advises, *"And whatsoever ye do, do it heartily, as to the Lord, and not unto men."* This verse encourages us to approach our tasks with dedication and purpose, enhancing our time management efforts.

Practical Exercise: Prioritized To-Do List

- **Instructions:**

    15. **List Tasks:** Write down all tasks you need to accomplish.
    16. **Prioritize:** Assign priority levels (e.g., high, medium, low) based on importance and urgency.
    17. **Allocate Time:** Schedule specific times for each high-priority task.

18. Review and Adjust: At the end of each day, review your progress and adjust your list for the next day.

Purpose: A prioritized to-do list ensures that you focus on what truly matters, reducing stress and enhancing productivity.

2. Cognitive Behavioral Techniques

Cognitive Behavioral Therapy (CBT) techniques help in identifying and challenging negative thought patterns, promoting a healthier mindset.

Personal Insight: Incorporating CBT techniques into my daily routine enabled me to recognize and reframe negative thoughts, fostering a more positive and resilient outlook on my healing journey.

Scriptural Insight: Philippians 4:8 (KJV) encourages positive thinking: *"Finally, brethren, whatsoever things are true, whatsoever things are honest, whatsoever things are just, whatsoever things are pure, whatsoever things are lovely, whatsoever things are of good report; if there be any virtue, and if there be any praise, think on these things."* This scripture aligns with CBT principles of focusing on positive thoughts to influence emotions and behaviors.

Practical Exercise: Thought Record Sheet

- **Instructions:**

19. Identify Negative Thought: Write down a negative or unhelpful thought.

20. **Challenge It:** Question the validity of the thought. Is it based on facts or assumptions?
21. **Reframe:** Replace the negative thought with a more positive and realistic one.
22. **Reflect:** Note how the reframed thought makes you feel.

Purpose: This exercise helps in transforming negative thought patterns, promoting emotional well-being and resilience.

3. Setting Boundaries

Establishing clear boundaries is essential for maintaining balance and protecting your well-being. Boundaries help you manage your time, energy, and emotional resources effectively.

Personal Insight: Setting boundaries at work and in personal relationships allowed me to prioritize my healing and prevent burnout. It ensured that I had the necessary space to focus on my well-being without external pressures.

Scriptural Insight: Galatians 6:2 (KJV) instructs, *"Bear ye one another's burdens, and so fulfil the law of Christ."* While this encourages support, it also implies the importance of not overextending oneself, maintaining healthy boundaries to sustain the ability to support others.

Practical Exercise: Boundary Setting Plan

• **Instructions:**

23. **Identify Needs:** Determine areas where boundaries are needed (e.g., work hours, personal time).

24. **Define Limits:** Clearly outline what is acceptable and what is not in each area.
25. **Communicate:** Inform relevant individuals about your boundaries respectfully and assertively.
26. **Enforce:** Consistently uphold your boundaries, making adjustments as necessary.

Purpose: A boundary setting plan ensures that you maintain control over your time and energy, fostering a balanced and sustainable healing process.

4. Utilizing Affirmations

Affirmations are positive statements that can reprogram your mind, reinforce self-belief, and promote a positive outlook.

Personal Insight: Reciting affirmations daily instilled a sense of confidence and positivity, helping me stay motivated and resilient throughout my healing journey.

Scriptural Insight: Proverbs 18:21 (KJV) states, *"Death and life are in the power of the tongue: and they that love it shall eat the fruit thereof."* This verse highlights the impact of our words on our lives, aligning with the practice of using affirmations to foster positive change.

Practical Exercise: Daily Affirmations

- **Instructions:**

27. **Create Affirmations:** Write down three positive affirmations that resonate with your healing goals (e.g., "I am strong and resilient,"

"I trust in God's plan for my healing," "Every day, I grow healthier and more at peace.").

28. **Recite Daily:** Repeat these affirmations each morning and evening.

29. **Visualize:** As you recite each affirmation, visualize yourself embodying these positive statements.

Purpose: Daily affirmations reinforce positive beliefs, enhance self-esteem, and support a resilient mindset during the healing process.

Section 4: Maintaining Progress Amidst Challenges

Sustaining progress in the face of ongoing challenges requires dedication, adaptability, and continuous self-care. It's essential to recognize that setbacks are a natural part of the healing journey and to develop strategies to navigate them effectively.

1. Embracing Flexibility

Flexibility allows you to adapt to changing circumstances and adjust your plans as needed. It prevents rigidity, enabling you to respond effectively to unexpected challenges.

Personal Insight: During my recovery, unforeseen complications required me to adjust my healing plan. Embracing flexibility allowed me to incorporate new therapies and adapt my schedule without feeling overwhelmed or defeated.

Scriptural Insight: Isaiah 55:8-9 (KJV) reminds us, *"For my thoughts are not your thoughts, neither are your ways my ways, saith the LORD. For as the heavens are higher than the earth, so are my ways higher than your ways, and my thoughts than your thoughts."* This scripture encourages trust in God's greater plan, fostering flexibility in our approach to challenges.

Practical Exercise: Flexible Goal Setting

- **Instructions:**

    30. **Set Goals:** Define specific, achievable goals for your healing journey.
    31. **Build in Flexibility:** Allow room for adjustments based on your progress and any unforeseen challenges.
    32. **Review Regularly:** Periodically assess your goals and make necessary changes to stay aligned with your healing needs.
    33. **Stay Adaptable:** Embrace changes as opportunities for growth rather than setbacks.

Purpose: Flexible goal setting ensures that you remain committed to your healing journey while accommodating the dynamic nature of life's challenges.

2. Celebrating Small Wins

Acknowledging and celebrating small victories boosts morale and reinforces positive behaviors. It provides motivation to continue striving toward larger goals.

Personal Insight: Celebrating minor milestones, such as completing a week of consistent prayer or achieving a personal best in physical therapy, kept me motivated and positive throughout my recovery.

Scriptural Insight: 1 Thessalonians 5:18 (KJV) advises, *"In every thing give thanks: for this is the will of God in Christ Jesus concerning you."* This scripture encourages gratitude, fostering a mindset that appreciates progress and blessings.

Practical Exercise: Victory Log

- **Instructions:**

    34. **Daily Entries:** Write down at least one small win each day related to your healing journey.
    35. **Reflect on Achievements:** Take time to appreciate and reflect on each victory.
    36. **Share Successes:** Share your small wins with your support network to receive encouragement and celebrate together.

Purpose: Keeping a victory log cultivates a positive outlook, reinforces progress, and maintains motivation during the healing process.

3. Managing Setbacks

Setbacks are inevitable, but how you respond to them determines the overall trajectory of your healing journey. Developing strategies to manage setbacks effectively is crucial for long-term success.

Personal Insight: Encountering setbacks, such as a temporary increase in pain or emotional distress, taught me patience and the importance of seeking support. Instead of feeling defeated, I used these moments to reassess my strategies and seek additional help when needed.

Scriptural Insight: Romans 5:3-4 (KJV) encourages perseverance: *"And not only so, but we glory in tribulations also: knowing that tribulation worketh patience; And patience, experience; and experience, hope."* This scripture highlights the growth that comes from enduring and overcoming challenges.

Practical Exercise: Setback Action Plan

- **Instructions:**

    37. **Identify Potential Setbacks:** List possible challenges you might encounter during your healing journey.
    38. **Develop Responses:** For each potential setback, outline specific steps to address and overcome it.
    39. **Stay Prepared:** Keep your action plan accessible, referring to it when setbacks occur.
    40. **Seek Support:** Reach out to your support network or professionals when facing significant setbacks.

Purpose: A setback action plan provides a proactive approach to managing challenges, ensuring that you remain resilient and focused on your healing goals.

Section 5: Inspirational Scriptures to Guide You

Throughout your healing journey, scriptures can serve as a source of strength, guidance, and encouragement. Reflecting on these verses can reinforce your faith and provide comfort during difficult times.

Isaiah 41:10 (KJV)

"Fear thou not; for I am with thee: be not dismayed; for I am thy God: I will strengthen thee; yea, I will help thee; yea, I will uphold thee with the right hand of my righteousness."

This scripture offers reassurance of God's presence and support, encouraging you to face challenges with courage and faith.

Psalm 46:1-2 (KJV)

"God is our refuge and strength, a very present help in trouble. Therefore will not we fear, though the earth be removed, and though the mountains be carried into the midst of the sea;"

These verses emphasize God's role as a steadfast protector and source of strength, inspiring confidence and trust during times of turmoil.

Joshua 1:9 (KJV)

"Have not I commanded thee? Be strong and of a good courage; be not afraid, neither be thou dismayed: for the LORD thy God is with thee whithersoever thou goest."

This scripture calls for strength and courage, reminding you of God's unwavering presence as you navigate your healing journey.

Romans 12:12 (KJV)

"Rejoicing in hope; patient in tribulation; continuing instant in prayer."

These verses highlight the importance of maintaining hope, patience, and a consistent prayer life, essential components for overcoming challenges.

Philippians 4:13 (KJV)

"I can do all things through Christ which strengtheneth me."

This powerful affirmation underscores the limitless strength available through faith, empowering you to overcome any obstacle.

Reflection Prompt: Choose one of these scriptures that resonates most with your current situation. Reflect on its meaning and how it can guide you through your challenges.

Conclusion: Persevering Through Adversity

Overcoming challenges and resistance is an integral part of the healing journey. By understanding the nature of resistance, implementing effective strategies, and drawing strength from your faith, you can navigate obstacles with resilience and grace. Remember that each challenge is an opportunity for growth, shaping you into a stronger and more compassionate individual.

As you continue on your path of healing and personal growth, let the words of Philippians 4:13 (KJV) resonate within you: *"I can do all things through Christ which strengtheneth me."* Embrace the challenges, lean on your faith, and trust in the divine strength that empowers you to overcome and thrive.

Practical Application

- **Exercise: Reflection and Action**

  o **Reflect:** Take time to meditate on the scriptures provided. Consider how each verse applies to your healing journey.

  o **Journal:** Write down your reflections, noting any insights or feelings that arise.

  o **Act:** Identify specific actions you can take to incorporate the lessons from these scriptures into your daily life.

  o **Share:** Discuss your reflections with a trusted friend, family member, or spiritual advisor to gain further insights and encouragement.

Purpose: This exercise deepens your connection to the scriptures, reinforces your commitment to overcoming challenges, and integrates spiritual insights into your healing process.

Final Encouragement

Healing and personal growth are ongoing processes, marked by both triumphs and trials. Embrace each moment with faith and resilience, knowing that with every challenge overcome, you move closer to a more fulfilled and strengthened self. Let your sacrifices be guided by purpose, your actions fueled by faith, and your spirit uplifted by the unwavering support of God and your community.

Prayer: "Heavenly Father, thank You for the strength and guidance You provide during my healing journey. Help me to embrace the challenges with courage and resilience, trusting in Your divine plan. Strengthen my spirit, renew my hope, and surround me with Your love and support. In Jesus' name, Amen."

CHAPTER 6

Practical Exercises for Personal Growth

Introduction: Active Engagement in Your Healing Journey

Personal growth is a proactive and intentional process that requires dedication, self-awareness, and consistent effort. It involves stepping out of your comfort zone, embracing change, and committing to continuous improvement. This chapter provides a series of practical exercises designed to reinforce the concepts discussed in previous chapters, enabling you to actively engage in your healing journey, embrace necessary sacrifices, and foster sustained personal development.

Scriptural Insight:

"But they that wait upon the LORD shall renew their strength; they shall mount up with wings as eagles; they shall run, and not be weary; and they shall walk, and not faint." – **Isaiah 40:31 (KJV)**

Reflection Prompt:

Reflect on the areas of your life that require active engagement for personal growth. How can the exercises in this chapter help you address these areas effectively?

Exercise 1: Goal Setting for Personal Growth

Purpose:

Setting clear and achievable goals provides direction and motivation, helping you focus your efforts on specific areas of personal growth.

Instructions:

1. **Identify Your Growth Areas:**

   o List the aspects of your life you wish to improve. These could be emotional, spiritual, relational, or professional.

   o *Example:* "Enhance my prayer life," "Improve my communication skills," "Develop healthier relationships."

2. Define SMART Goals:

- o **Specific:** Clearly define what you want to achieve.
- o **Measurable:** Ensure you can track your progress.
- o **Achievable:** Set realistic goals that are attainable.
- o **Relevant:** Align your goals with your overall personal growth objectives.
- o **Time-bound:** Set a deadline for achieving your goals.
- o *Example:* "I will dedicate 15 minutes each morning to prayer and scripture reading for the next 30 days."

3. Break Down Goals into Action Steps:

- o Divide each goal into smaller, manageable tasks.
- o *Example:* For improving communication skills:
  - Read a book on effective communication.
  - Practice active listening in daily conversations.
  - Seek feedback from trusted friends or mentors.

4. Create a Timeline:

- o Assign specific deadlines to each action step to maintain momentum.
- o *Example:* "Read one chapter of the communication book each week."

5. Monitor and Adjust:

- o Regularly review your progress and make necessary adjustments to your goals or action steps.

o   *Example:* "If I find the daily prayer time challenging, adjust it to early evening."

Scriptural Reinforcement:

"Commit thy works unto the LORD, and thy thoughts shall be established." – **Proverbs 16:3 (KJV)**

Personal Insight:

Setting SMART goals has been transformative in my personal growth journey. It provides clarity and a sense of purpose, ensuring that my efforts are aligned with my spiritual and personal aspirations.

Exercise 2: Gratitude Journaling

Purpose:

Practicing gratitude shifts your focus from what you lack to what you have, fostering a positive mindset and enhancing emotional well-being.

Instructions:

1. **Choose Your Journal:**

   o   Select a dedicated notebook or digital document for your gratitude entries.

2. **Daily Entries:**

   o   Each day, write down at least three things you are grateful for.
   o   Be specific and reflect on why you are thankful for each item.
   o   *Example:* "I am grateful for the supportive conversation I had with my friend today because it uplifted my spirits."

3. **Reflect on Your Entries:**

   o   At the end of each week, review your gratitude entries.
   o   Identify patterns or recurring themes that highlight what brings you joy and contentment.

4. **Incorporate Scriptures:**

   o   Include relevant scriptures that reinforce the practice of gratitude.
   o   *Example: "In every thing give thanks: for this is the will of God in Christ Jesus concerning you."* – **1 Thessalonians 5:18 (KJV)**

Scriptural Reinforcement:

"Give thanks in all circumstances: for this is the will of God in Christ Jesus concerning you." – **1 Thessalonians 5:18 (KJV)**

Personal Insight:

Gratitude journaling has significantly impacted my outlook on life. It cultivates a heart of thankfulness, reminding me of God's blessings even during challenging times.

Exercise 3: Mindfulness Meditation

Purpose:

Mindfulness meditation enhances self-awareness, reduces stress, and fosters a deeper connection with your inner self and faith.

Instructions:

1. **Find a Quiet Space:**

   o Choose a comfortable and quiet environment where you can meditate without interruptions.

2. **Set a Time Limit:**

   o Start with 5-10 minutes and gradually increase the duration as you become more comfortable.

3. **Focus on Your Breath:**

   o Close your eyes and take deep breaths, focusing on the sensation of inhaling and exhaling.

o Let go of any distracting thoughts and gently bring your focus back to your breath when your mind wanders.

4. Incorporate Scripture:

o Meditate on a specific scripture verse that resonates with your current state of mind.
o *Example: "Be still, and know that I am God." –* **Psalm 46:10 (KJV)**

5. Reflect Post-Meditation:

o Spend a few minutes reflecting on your meditation experience.
o Journal any insights or feelings that arose during the practice.

Scriptural Reinforcement:

"Be still, and know that I am God." – **Psalm 46:10 (KJV)**

Personal Insight:

Mindfulness meditation has deepened my spiritual connection and provided clarity during moments of uncertainty. It serves as a spiritual retreat, allowing me to center myself and seek divine guidance.

Exercise 4: Acts of Service

Purpose:

Engaging in acts of service fosters compassion, strengthens community bonds, and aligns your actions with your faith.

Instructions:

1. **Identify Service Opportunities:**

   o   Look for ways to serve others in your community, church, or personal network.

   o   *Example:* Volunteering at a local food bank, visiting the elderly, or assisting in church activities.

2. **Commit to Regular Service:**

   o   Schedule regular times to perform acts of service.

   o   *Example:* "Volunteer at the food bank every second Saturday of the month."

3. **Reflect on Your Experiences:**

   o   After each act of service, take time to reflect on how it impacted you and those you served.

   o   Journal your experiences and any lessons learned.

4. **Incorporate Scripture:**

   o   Meditate on scriptures that emphasize the importance of serving others.

o *Example: "And whosoever will be chief among you, let him be your servant." –* **Matthew 20:26 (KJV)**

Scriptural Reinforcement:

"And whosoever will be chief among you, let him be your servant." – **Matthew 20:26 (KJV)**

Personal Insight:

Acts of service have enriched my life by allowing me to connect with others and fulfill Christ's command to serve. It cultivates humility and deepens my understanding of compassion.

Exercise 5: Affirmations and Positive Self-Talk

Purpose:

Affirmations and positive self-talk counteract negative thoughts, build self-esteem, and reinforce a positive self-image aligned with your faith.

Instructions:

1. **Create Affirmations:**

   o Develop positive statements that reflect your goals and affirm your worth.
   o *Example:* "I am strong in Christ," "I am worthy of love and respect."

2. **Daily Repetition:**

   o Recite your affirmations each morning and evening.
   o *Example:* "Today, I choose to embrace the strength that God provides."

3. **Visualize Success:**

   o As you recite your affirmations, visualize yourself achieving your goals and embodying the positive traits you affirm.
   o *Example:* Visualize confidently communicating with others or maintaining emotional stability.

4. **Incorporate Scripture:**

   o Align your affirmations with relevant scripture to reinforce their validity.
   o *Example:* "I can do all things through Christ which strengtheneth me." – **Philippians 4:13 (KJV)**

Scriptural Reinforcement:

"I can do all things through Christ which strengtheneth me." – **Philippians 4:13 (KJV)**

Personal Insight:

Using affirmations has transformed my internal dialogue, replacing self-doubt with confidence and aligning my thoughts with God's promises.

Exercise 6: Reflective Journaling

Purpose:

Reflective journaling enhances self-awareness, tracks progress, and provides a space for processing emotions and experiences.

Instructions:

1. **Choose Your Journal:**

   o   Select a dedicated notebook or digital document for your reflections.

2. **Set a Routine:**

   o   Allocate specific times each day or week for journaling.

   o   *Example:* "Write in my journal every night before bed."

3. **Prompt Your Reflections:**

   o   Use guided prompts to explore your thoughts and feelings.

   o   *Example:* "What did I learn about myself today?" "How did I see God's hand in my challenges?"

4. **Incorporate Scriptures:**

   o   Include relevant scriptures that resonate with your reflections.

o *Example: "The LORD is my shepherd; I shall not want." –* **Psalm 23:1 (KJV)**

5. Review and Reflect:

o Periodically review your journal entries to identify patterns, growth, and areas needing attention.

o *Example:* "Notice recurring themes of gratitude and strength in my entries."

Scriptural Reinforcement:

"The LORD is my shepherd; I shall not want." – **Psalm 23:1 (KJV)**

Personal Insight:

Reflective journaling has provided me with clarity and insight into my personal growth journey. It serves as a record of God's faithfulness and my evolving relationship with Him.

Exercise 7: Accountability Partnerships

Purpose:

Accountability partnerships provide mutual support, encouragement, and accountability, enhancing your commitment to personal growth goals.

Instructions:

1. Identify an Accountability Partner:

- o Choose a trusted friend, family member, or mentor who shares your commitment to personal growth.
- o *Example:* "Partner with a fellow church member who is also focused on spiritual growth."

2. Set Regular Meetings:

- o Schedule consistent times to meet and discuss your progress.
- o *Example:* "Meet bi-weekly to share updates and provide support."

3. Share Your Goals:

- o Openly discuss your personal growth goals and the steps you are taking to achieve them.
- o *Example:* "Share my goal to improve communication skills and seek feedback."

4. Provide and Receive Feedback:

- o Offer constructive feedback and encouragement to each other.
- o *Example:* "Encourage each other to stay committed to daily affirmations."

5. **Pray Together:**

   o Incorporate prayer into your meetings to seek divine guidance and strength.
   o *Example:* "Pray for each other's goals and challenges."

Scriptural Reinforcement:

"Iron sharpeneth iron; so a man sharpeneth the countenance of his friend." – **Proverbs 27:17 (KJV)**

Personal Insight:

Having an accountability partner has been invaluable in my personal growth journey. It provides a sense of responsibility and the encouragement needed to stay committed to my goals.

Exercise 8: Self-Care Practices

Purpose:

Engaging in self-care promotes physical, emotional, and spiritual well-being, essential for sustaining personal growth and healing.

Instructions:

1. **Identify Self-Care Activities:**

   o List activities that nourish your body, mind, and spirit.

o   *Example:* "Exercise, adequate sleep, healthy eating, prayer, meditation."

2. Create a Self-Care Schedule:

o   Allocate specific times for self-care activities in your daily or weekly routine.

o   *Example:* "Exercise every morning, meditate every evening."

3. Set Boundaries:

o   Establish boundaries to protect your time and energy for self-care.

o   *Example:* "Limit work hours to prevent burnout and ensure time for rest."

4. Incorporate Faith-Based Self-Care:

o   Engage in spiritual practices that enhance your connection with God.

o   *Example:* "Read a devotional each day, attend church services regularly."

5. Reflect on Your Self-Care:

o   Regularly assess the effectiveness of your self-care practices and make adjustments as needed.

o   *Example:* "Evaluate how daily exercise impacts my mood and energy levels."

Scriptural Reinforcement:

"Come unto me, all ye that labour and are heavy laden, and I will give you rest." – **Matthew 11:28 (KJV)**

Personal Insight:

Prioritizing self-care has significantly improved my overall well-being, enabling me to better support my personal growth and fulfill my responsibilities with greater energy and enthusiasm.

Exercise 9: Visualization Techniques

Purpose:

Visualization techniques help you mentally rehearse achieving your goals, enhancing motivation and clarity.

Instructions:

1. **Find a Quiet Space:**

   o   Choose a comfortable and quiet environment where you can visualize without distractions.

2. **Set an Intention:**

   o   Clearly define what you want to visualize.
   o   *Example:* "Visualize myself confidently communicating in social settings."

3. **Engage Your Senses:**

   o Imagine the sights, sounds, smells, and feelings associated with achieving your goal.

   o *Example:* "See myself smiling and engaging in meaningful conversations, hear the positive feedback, feel the sense of accomplishment."

4. **Incorporate Scripture:**

   o Meditate on scriptures that support your visualization.

   o *Example: "For God hath not given us the spirit of fear; but of power, and of love, and of a sound mind." –* **2 Timothy 1:7 (KJV)**

5. **Regular Practice:**

   o Dedicate time each day to practice visualization, reinforcing your commitment to your goals.

   o *Example:* "Spend five minutes each morning visualizing my goals."

Scriptural Reinforcement:

"For God hath not given us the spirit of fear; but of power, and of love, and of a sound mind." – **2 Timothy 1:7 (KJV)**

Personal Insight:

Visualization has empowered me to see my goals clearly and feel confident in my ability to achieve them. It bridges the gap between where I am and where I aspire to be.

Exercise 10: Forgiveness Practice

Purpose:

Practicing forgiveness releases emotional burdens, promotes healing, and fosters healthier relationships, essential for personal growth.

Instructions:

1. Identify Hurts:

o   Reflect on past hurts or grievances that you need to forgive.

o   *Example:* "Forgive a friend who betrayed my trust."

2. Acknowledge Your Emotions:

o   Recognize and validate the feelings associated with the hurt.

o   *Example:* "Feelings of anger, sadness, or disappointment."

3. Seek Divine Guidance:

o   Pray for the strength and wisdom to forgive.

o   *Example:* "Pray for the ability to let go of resentment and embrace forgiveness."

4. Release the Hurt:

o Make a conscious decision to forgive, letting go of negative emotions.

o *Example:* "Say a prayer of forgiveness, releasing the grudge held against the person."

5. Reflect on the Benefits:

o Consider how forgiveness contributes to your emotional and spiritual well-being.

o *Example:* "Feel a sense of peace and freedom after forgiving."

Scriptural Reinforcement:

"And be ye kind one to another, tenderhearted, forgiving one another, even as God for Christ's sake hath forgiven you." – **Ephesians 4:32 (KJV)**

Personal Insight:

Forgiveness has been a transformative practice in my healing journey. It has liberated me from past pain and allowed me to move forward with a lighter heart and a renewed spirit.

Conclusion

Engaging in practical exercises is essential for translating the concepts of healing, sacrifice, and personal growth into tangible actions. These exercises empower you to take active steps toward your transformation, fostering sustained growth and deeper spiritual connection. By integrating these practices into your daily life, you reinforce your commitment to healing and embrace the sacrifices necessary for profound personal development.

Scriptural Reinforcement:

"And let us not be weary in well doing: for in due season we shall reap, if we faint not." – **Galatians 6:9 (KJV)**

Final Prayer for the Chapter:

"Heavenly Father, thank You for providing these practical exercises to guide my personal growth journey. Help me to commit to these practices with dedication and faith, trusting that You are renewing my strength and guiding me toward healing and transformation. Grant me the perseverance to continue well doing, knowing that in due season I shall reap the rewards of my efforts. In Jesus' name, Amen."

CHAPTER 7

—

Building a Support System

In the journey of healing and personal growth, the significance of a strong support system cannot be overstated. Just as the body relies on its veins to circulate life-sustaining blood, our emotional and spiritual well-being thrives on the connections we cultivate with others. Building a support system is a deliberate and sacrificial act, requiring us to invest time, energy, and often, to let go of relationships that no longer serve our highest good. This chapter delves into the importance of creating and nurturing a network of support that aligns with our path of healing and growth.

"Two are better than one; because they have a good reward for their labour. For if they fall, the one will lift up his fellow: but woe to him that is alone when he falleth; for he hath not another to help him up." – **Ecclesiastes 4:9-10 (KJV)**

This scripture beautifully encapsulates the essence of a support system. It highlights the strength found in companionship and the mutual benefits that arise from supportive relationships. In times of struggle, having someone to lean on can make all the difference between faltering and forging ahead.

Reflecting on my own journey, I recall a period of intense personal turmoil where the weight of unresolved emotions and unhealed wounds felt unbearable. It was during this time that the value of a supportive network became profoundly evident. Friends who listened without judgment, family members who offered unwavering encouragement, and mentors who provided wise counsel were instrumental in my healing process. Their presence not only provided comfort but also offered different perspectives that helped me navigate through my darkest moments.

Reflection Prompt:

Consider the relationships in your life. Who are the individuals that consistently support and uplift you? How have these relationships contributed to your healing and personal growth?

Building a support system begins with identifying those who genuinely care for your well-being. These individuals are often the ones who demonstrate empathy, offer constructive feedback, and encourage your pursuit of healing and growth. However, building such a network also involves a level of sacrifice. It may require distancing yourself from relationships that are toxic or draining, even if they were once close. This act of letting go is a form of self-sacrifice, prioritizing your health and growth over maintaining potentially harmful connections.

Practical Exercise: Support Network Mapping

1. **Identify Your Supportive Individuals:**

   Begin by listing the people in your life who have consistently shown support, understanding, and encouragement. These could be friends, family members, mentors, or members of your faith community.

   Example: "List three friends who always listen without judgment, a family member who offers unwavering support, and a mentor who provides wise counsel."

2. **Assess the Quality of Support:**

   Evaluate the type of support each individual provides. Understanding their unique contributions can help you leverage their strengths effectively.

   Example: "Determine which friends offer emotional support, which provide practical assistance, and which offer spiritual guidance."

3. **Strengthen Existing Connections:**

   Invest time and effort in nurturing these relationships. This could involve regular check-ins, shared activities, or simply expressing gratitude for their support.

   Example: "Schedule a weekly coffee date with a supportive friend to maintain and deepen your connection."

4. **Expand Your Support Network:**

Seek out new relationships that align with your goals and values. Joining groups, attending workshops, or participating in community activities can introduce you to individuals who can contribute positively to your growth.

Example: "Join a local church group or a personal development workshop to meet like-minded individuals."

5. **Offer Support in Return:**

A support system thrives on mutual assistance. Be willing to offer your support to others, creating a reciprocal and balanced network.

Example: "Offer to help a friend in need or provide encouragement to a colleague facing challenges."

Building a support system is not a one-time task but an ongoing process. It requires continuous effort to maintain and strengthen these relationships. As you grow and evolve, your support network should adapt to meet your changing needs. This dynamic process ensures that you remain connected to those who truly matter and who contribute positively to your healing and growth.

Personal Insight:

In my experience, the most profound growth occurs within a supportive community. Being part of a group that shares similar values and goals fosters a sense of belonging and accountability. For instance, participating in a Bible study group not only deepens my spiritual understanding but also connects me with individuals who inspire and challenge me to grow. These relationships provide a safe space to share vulnerabilities, celebrate successes, and navigate setbacks together.

However, building a support system also means recognizing when certain relationships hinder your progress. There was a time when I maintained a friendship that, while longstanding, consistently left me feeling drained and unsupported. Choosing to distance myself was a difficult but necessary sacrifice. It opened up space for more nurturing and uplifting relationships that better aligned with my healing journey.

Reflection Prompt:

Identify any relationships that may be hindering your personal growth. What steps can you take to address these relationships, and how might doing so benefit your healing journey?

Creating a supportive network also involves seeking guidance and mentorship. Mentors play a crucial role in personal growth by offering wisdom, accountability, and a broader perspective. They can help you set realistic goals, overcome obstacles, and stay committed to your path of healing. Seeking out mentors within your faith community or professional circles can provide invaluable support and direction.

Practical Exercise: Seeking Mentorship

1. Identify Potential Mentors:

Look for individuals who exemplify the qualities you aspire to develop. These could be leaders within your community, experienced professionals, or spiritual guides.

Example: "List individuals who have successfully navigated similar healing journeys or who embody the virtues you admire."

2. Reach Out:

Approach these individuals with humility and a clear intention. Express your desire for guidance and support in your personal growth journey.

Example: "Send a heartfelt message or request a meeting to discuss your aspirations and seek their mentorship."

3. Establish a Mentorship Relationship:

Clearly define the expectations and boundaries of the mentorship. This includes the frequency of meetings, the areas of focus, and the nature of the support provided.

Example: "Agree to meet monthly to review progress, discuss challenges, and set new goals."

4. Engage Actively:

Take an active role in the mentorship by being open to feedback, implementing advice, and showing appreciation for their support.

Example: "Apply the strategies discussed in your mentorship meetings and provide updates on your progress."

Scriptural Reinforcement:

"Iron sharpeneth iron; so a man sharpeneth the countenance of his friend." – **Proverbs 27:17 (KJV)**

Personal Insight:

The presence of a mentor in my life has been transformative. Their guidance has not only helped me set and achieve meaningful goals but has also provided a sense of accountability that keeps me committed to my healing journey. Their experiences and insights have offered me a roadmap to navigate challenges that I might have otherwise struggled to overcome alone.

Building a support system also means fostering a sense of community. Engaging with others who are on similar healing and growth paths can provide a sense of solidarity and shared purpose. This communal support can amplify the benefits of individual relationships, creating a network of encouragement and mutual upliftment.

Practical Exercise: Building Community Connections

1. **Join Support Groups:**

   Participate in support groups or communities that focus on healing and personal growth. These groups offer a space to share experiences, gain insights, and receive encouragement from others facing similar challenges.

   Example: "Attend a weekly support group meeting focused on emotional healing or join an online community dedicated to personal development."

2. **Participate in Community Events:**

   Engage in events and activities that promote personal growth and community building. This could include workshops, retreats, seminars, or volunteer opportunities.

   Example: "Enroll in a personal development workshop or volunteer at a local charity to meet new people and expand your support network."

3. **Foster Group Activities:**

   Initiate or participate in group activities that encourage bonding and mutual support. This could involve book clubs, prayer groups, or hobby-based gatherings.

   Example: "Start a monthly book club focused on spiritual and personal growth literature or join a local hiking group to combine physical activity with social interaction."

4. Encourage Inclusivity and Diversity:

Embrace diversity within your support system by including individuals from various backgrounds and perspectives. This enriches your network and broadens your understanding of different healing and growth experiences.

Example: "Invite people from different walks of life to join your support group, fostering a richer and more diverse community."

Scriptural Reinforcement:

"Bear ye one another's burdens, and so fulfil the law of Christ." – **Galatians 6:2 (KJV)**

Personal Insight:

Engaging with a community has deepened my sense of belonging and provided a wellspring of support that individual relationships alone cannot offer. The collective wisdom and shared experiences within a community create a nurturing environment that fosters sustained healing and growth. Being part of a community also reinforces the idea that I am not alone in my struggles, providing comfort and encouragement during challenging times.

Building a support system is intrinsically linked to our faith. Our spiritual beliefs often shape our values, goals, and the way we interact with others. Integrating faith into your support system ensures that your relationships are rooted in shared beliefs and mutual respect for each other's spiritual journeys.

Practical Exercise: Integrating Faith into Your Support System

1. Attend Faith-Based Gatherings:

Participate in church services, Bible studies, prayer meetings, or other faith-based activities that connect you with like-minded individuals.

Example: "Join a weekly Bible study group to deepen your spiritual understanding and connect with others who share your faith."

2. Share Your Faith Journey:

Openly discuss your faith journey with your support network, allowing others to understand your spiritual motivations and aspirations.

Example: "Share personal testimonies during group meetings to inspire and encourage others in their faith and healing journeys."

3. Encourage Faith Practices:

Engage in shared faith practices with your support network, such as praying together, reading scriptures, or worshiping as a group.

Example: "Organize a weekly prayer session with your support group to foster spiritual growth and mutual encouragement."

4. Seek Spiritual Guidance:

Incorporate spiritual guidance and mentorship within your support system, seeking advice and wisdom from spiritually mature individuals.

Example: "Consult with a pastor or spiritual mentor when facing significant challenges or decisions in your healing journey."

Scriptural Reinforcement:

"And above all things have fervent charity among yourselves: for charity shall cover the multitude of sins." – **1 Peter 4:8 (KJV)**

Personal Insight:

Integrating faith into my support system has provided a strong foundation for my healing and growth. Shared faith practices not only strengthen my spiritual connection but also create a unified purpose among my support network. This spiritual alignment fosters deeper relationships and a collective resilience that sustains us through individual and shared challenges.

Building a support system is a testament to the power of community and the importance of surrounding ourselves with those who uplift and encourage us. It is a journey that requires intentionality, sacrifice, and a commitment to nurturing meaningful relationships. By investing in a robust support network, you create a safety net that catches you during times of need and propels you forward in your healing and personal growth journey.

Reflection Prompt:

How can you intentionally invest in your current relationships to strengthen your support system? What new connections can you seek to enhance your network of support?

Scriptural Reinforcement:

"For where two or three are gathered together in my name, there am I in the midst of them." – **Matthew 18:20 (KJV)**

Personal Insight:

The presence of a strong support system has been instrumental in my journey of healing and personal growth. It provides not only practical assistance but also emotional and spiritual encouragement that fuels my resilience and determination. Recognizing the value of these relationships has inspired me to continually seek and nurture connections that align with my path of healing and growth.

In conclusion, building a support system is a vital component of healing and personal growth. It involves identifying and nurturing relationships that offer genuine support, seeking mentorship, fostering a sense of community, and integrating faith into your connections. This intentional investment in meaningful relationships provides the foundation for sustained healing, resilience, and profound personal transformation.

"Iron sharpeneth iron; so a man sharpeneth the countenance of his friend." – **Proverbs 27:17 (KJV)**

As you embark on building or strengthening your support system, remember that these relationships are not only beneficial for your healing journey but also an opportunity to uplift and support others in their paths. Embrace the collective strength found in a supportive network, and allow these connections to guide you toward lasting healing and personal growth.

Final Prayer for the Chapter:

"Heavenly Father, thank You for the gift of community and the supportive relationships that sustain me in my healing journey. Help me to build and nurture connections that align with Your will, fostering an environment of love, encouragement, and mutual growth. Grant me the wisdom to seek out and cherish those who uplift me, and the strength to offer the same support to others. In Jesus' name, Amen."

CHAPTER 8

Embracing Transformation and Moving Forward

Introduction: Stepping into a New Chapter

Transformation is the culmination of a journey marked by sacrifice, healing, and personal growth. It signifies a profound shift in identity, mindset, and behavior, leading to a more fulfilled and purposeful life. Embracing transformation means not only recognizing the changes within yourself but also actively moving forward with confidence and resilience. This chapter explores the essential elements of transformation, offering guidance on how to integrate your newfound self into every aspect of your life, ensuring sustained growth and meaningful progress.

"Therefore if any man be in Christ, he is a new creature: old things are passed away; behold, all things are become new."– **2 Corinthians 5:17 (KJV)**

Reflection Prompt: Reflect on the changes you've experienced so far. How do these transformations align with your spiritual beliefs and personal goals?

Understanding Transformation

True transformation is holistic, impacting every facet of our being—physical, emotional, mental, and spiritual. It involves a fundamental shift in how we perceive ourselves and the world, leading to lasting change. Transformation is not merely about changing behaviors or adopting new habits; it's about renewing your entire identity in alignment with your faith and values.

"And be not conformed to this world: but be ye transformed by the renewing of your mind, that ye may prove what is that good, and acceptable, and perfect, will of God." – **Romans 12:2 (KJV)**

Personal Insight: My own transformation journey revealed that true change begins internally. By renewing my mind and healing emotionally, I noticed tangible improvements in my behavior and spiritual practices, ensuring a comprehensive and enduring transformation.

Reflection Prompt: What internal changes have you experienced that signify your transformation? How do these changes reflect your alignment with your spiritual beliefs?

Integrating Your New Identity

Integration involves ensuring that your daily actions, decisions, and habits reflect your new identity. It's about living authentically and consistently with the person you have become. This process requires conscious effort to align your lifestyle with your transformed self, fostering a harmonious and balanced existence.

"That ye put off concerning the former conversation the old man, which is corrupt according to the deceitful lusts; And be renewed in the spirit of your mind; And that ye put on the new man, which after God is created in righteousness and true holiness." – **Ephesians 4:22-24 (KJV)**

Personal Insight: Aligning my actions with my transformed self meant making conscious choices that reflected my renewed values and purpose. Whether it was in my career, relationships, or personal habits, each decision became a testament to my ongoing growth and commitment.

Reflection Prompt: How do your daily actions reflect your transformed self? Are there areas where you feel your actions could better align with your new identity?

Building Resilience Through Transformation

Resilience is the ability to recover from setbacks and continue moving forward. Transformation strengthens resilience by equipping you with the tools to handle challenges with grace and perseverance. Building emotional and spiritual resilience ensures that you remain steadfast in your journey, even when faced with adversity.

"Blessed is the man that endureth temptation: for when he is tried, he shall receive the crown of life, which the Lord hath promised to them that love him." – **James 1:12 (KJV)**

Personal Insight: Embracing transformation has significantly boosted my resilience. By cultivating a deeper connection with my faith and adopting healthier coping mechanisms, I've become better equipped to navigate life's inevitable challenges.

Reflection Prompt: In what ways has your transformation journey strengthened your ability to handle life's challenges? How can you further cultivate resilience in your ongoing growth?

Moving Forward with Confidence

Transformation often involves embracing change and navigating uncertainty. Moving forward with confidence means trusting in the process and believing in your ability to thrive in new circumstances. It requires letting go of fear and embracing the unknown with faith and optimism.

"Trust in the LORD with all thine heart; and lean not unto thine own understanding. In all thy ways acknowledge him, and he shall direct thy paths." – **Proverbs 3:5-6 (KJV)**

Personal Insight: Accepting that change is a natural part of life has empowered me to approach uncertainty with optimism. Trusting in my journey and the lessons learned along the way has been key to maintaining confidence and enthusiasm for the future.

Reflection Prompt: How do you handle change and uncertainty in your life? What steps can you take to embrace these aspects with greater confidence and faith?

Sustaining Your Transformation

Sustaining transformation requires ongoing effort and dedication. It involves continuously nurturing your growth, staying connected to your support systems, and remaining committed to your values and goals. Maintaining momentum ensures that the changes you've embraced become enduring aspects of your life.

"I can do all things through Christ which strengtheneth me." – **Philippians 4:13 (KJV)**

Personal Insight: To maintain momentum in my transformation, I established regular check-ins with my support network and set ongoing personal development goals. This consistent effort ensured that my growth remained steady and aligned with my aspirations.

Reflection Prompt: What practices can you implement to ensure that your transformation remains ongoing and sustainable? How can you stay motivated and committed to your growth?

Embracing Your New Identity

Embracing transformation means living authentically, aligning your actions and choices with your true self. It involves shedding old identities that no longer serve you and stepping into the person you are becoming. Living authentically fosters inner peace and attracts meaningful relationships and opportunities.

"That ye put off concerning the former conversation the old man, which is corrupt according to the deceitful lusts; And be renewed in the spirit of your mind; And that ye put on the new man, which after God is created in righteousness and true holiness." – **Ephesians 4:22-24 (KJV)**

Personal Insight: Living authentically required me to let go of societal expectations and embrace my true desires and values. This authenticity not only brought inner peace but also attracted meaningful relationships and opportunities.

Reflection Prompt: In what ways can you live more authentically in your daily life? What old identities or expectations do you need to release to embrace your new self fully?

Embracing Community and Relationships

Transformation thrives within the context of supportive relationships and a strong community. Building meaningful connections provides encouragement, accountability, and shared wisdom on your journey. A robust support system enhances your resilience and sustains your personal growth.

"Two are better than one; because they have a good reward for their labour. For if they fall, the one will lift up his fellow: but woe to him that is alone when he falleth; for he hath not another to help him up." – **Ecclesiastes 4:9-10 (KJV)**

Personal Insight: Surrounding myself with a supportive community has been instrumental in my transformation. Sharing experiences and receiving encouragement from others has deepened my sense of belonging and reinforced my commitment to personal growth.

Reflection Prompt: How can you cultivate deeper, more meaningful relationships to support your ongoing transformation? What role does community play in your healing journey?

Navigating Life's Transitions

Life is a series of transitions, each presenting opportunities for growth and transformation. Adapting to these changes with grace and resilience ensures that your journey remains dynamic and fulfilling. Embracing transitions as part of your transformation journey allows you to grow in unexpected ways.

"For I know the thoughts that I think toward you, saith the LORD, thoughts of peace, and not of evil, to give you an expected end." – **Jeremiah 29:11 (KJV)**

Personal Insight: Navigating major life transitions, such as career changes or relocations, required me to remain flexible and open to new possibilities. Embracing these changes as part of my transformation journey allowed me to grow in unexpected ways.

Reflection Prompt: How do you handle major life transitions? What strategies can you employ to adapt more effectively and view these changes as opportunities for growth?

Maintaining Spiritual Alignment

Maintaining spiritual alignment is crucial for sustaining transformation. It involves regular practices that keep you connected to your faith and spiritual beliefs, providing guidance and strength. Spiritual alignment ensures that your transformation is grounded in your faith, fostering a deeper sense of purpose and direction.

"But they that wait upon the LORD shall renew their strength; they shall mount up with wings as eagles; they shall run, and not be weary; and they shall walk, and not faint." – **Isaiah 40:31 (KJV)**

Personal Insight: Consistent spiritual practices, such as prayer and scripture study, have been the foundation of my transformation. They provide clarity, peace, and a sense of purpose that guides my actions and decisions.

Reflection Prompt: What spiritual practices help you stay aligned with your faith and support your transformation? How can you incorporate these practices more consistently into your daily life?

Celebrating Milestones and Achievements

Celebrating milestones and achievements is essential for maintaining motivation and recognizing the progress you've made on your transformation journey. It reinforces your commitment and provides positive reinforcement, encouraging you to continue striving for growth.

"Let us rejoice and be exceeding glad: for great is your reward in heaven." – **Matthew 5:12 (KJV)**

Personal Insight: Celebrating small victories, such as overcoming a challenging habit or reaching a personal goal, has kept me motivated and encouraged me to continue striving for growth.

Reflection Prompt: What milestones have you achieved in your transformation journey? How can you celebrate these achievements to reinforce your progress and motivation?

Setting Future Goals

Setting future goals ensures that your transformation remains a dynamic and ongoing process. It provides direction and purpose, guiding your actions and decisions toward continued growth. Future goals act as a roadmap, helping you navigate your path with clarity and intention.

"For I know the thoughts that I think toward you, saith the LORD, thoughts of peace, and not of evil, to give you an expected end." – **Jeremiah 29:11 (KJV)**

Personal Insight: Establishing clear, achievable goals has kept me focused and driven in my transformation journey. It provides a roadmap for where I want to go and the steps I need to take to get there.

Reflection Prompt: What are your future goals for personal growth and transformation? How do these goals align with your faith and values?

Inspirational Tips for Integrating Faith Seamlessly

Integrating faith seamlessly into your daily life enhances your transformation journey by providing spiritual support, guidance, and strength. Blending faith with everyday activities ensures that your spiritual beliefs remain a central aspect of your personal growth and healing.

"Commit thy works unto the LORD, and thy thoughts shall be established." – **Proverbs 16:3 (KJV)**

Personal Insight: Incorporating faith into everyday activities has deepened my sense of purpose and provided continuous inspiration. Whether through morning prayers, scripture readings, or faith-based reflections, my daily life is enriched by my spiritual practices.

Reflection Prompt: How can you integrate your faith more seamlessly into your daily routines and activities? What specific practices can help you maintain a strong spiritual connection throughout the day?

Conclusion: Embracing Your New Self with Faith and Purpose

Transformation is not an endpoint but a continuous journey of growth, resilience, and alignment with your true self and divine purpose. By embracing the changes within you, integrating your new identity, building resilience, navigating life's transitions, maintaining spiritual alignment, celebrating achievements, setting future goals, and seamlessly integrating faith into your daily life, you create a life that is not only fulfilling and purposeful but also a testament to the power of sacrifice and healing.

"For I know the thoughts that I think toward you, saith the LORD, thoughts of peace, and not of evil, to give you an expected end." – **Jeremiah 29:11 (KJV)**

Final Prayer: "Heavenly Father, thank You for guiding me through my transformation journey. Help me to embrace the changes within me and move forward with confidence and faith. Strengthen my resolve to maintain my growth, and bless me with the resilience to navigate life's uncertainties. May my transformation honor You and inspire those around me. In Jesus' name, Amen."

CHAPTER 9

Sustaining Your Transformation

Introduction: Maintaining the Momentum of Change

Embarking on a journey of healing and personal growth is a monumental step towards a more fulfilling and purposeful life. However, transformation is not a finite event but a continuous process that requires ongoing commitment, dedication, and intentional effort. Sustaining your transformation ensures that the positive changes you've embraced become enduring aspects of your character and lifestyle. This chapter delves into strategies and practices that help maintain the momentum of your transformation, ensuring that your growth is not only achieved but also preserved over time.

"Let us not be weary in well doing: for in due season we shall reap, if we faint not." – **Galatians 6:9 (KJV)**

Reflection Prompt:

Reflect on the progress you've made in your transformation journey. What practices have been most effective in maintaining your growth, and how can you build upon them to ensure continued progress?

Understanding the Nature of Sustained Transformation

Sustained transformation involves integrating the changes you've made into every facet of your life, making them habitual and reflective of your true self. It requires a balance between maintaining the progress you've achieved and remaining open to further growth and development. Understanding that transformation is an ongoing journey helps set realistic expectations and fosters a mindset geared towards continuous improvement.

"For I know the thoughts that I think toward you, saith the LORD, thoughts of peace, and not of evil, to give you an expected end." – **Jeremiah 29:11 (KJV)**

Personal Insight:

Throughout my transformation journey, I've realized that sustaining change is as much about mindset as it is about actions. Embracing a growth mindset, where challenges are viewed as opportunities for further development, has been crucial in maintaining the progress I've made.

Reflection Prompt:

How do you perceive challenges and setbacks in your journey of transformation? How can adopting a growth mindset help you navigate these obstacles and sustain your progress?

Strategies for Sustaining Transformation

1. Continuous Learning and Adaptation

Transformation thrives on continuous learning. Engaging in lifelong learning ensures that you remain adaptable and open to new experiences, ideas, and perspectives that can further your personal growth.

"A wise man will hear, and will increase learning; and a man of understanding shall attain unto wise counsels." – **Proverbs 1:5 (KJV)**

Practical Exercise: Personal Development Plan

Instructions:

1. **Identify Learning Goals:**

   o Determine areas where you seek further knowledge or skills.
   o *Example:* "Learn effective communication techniques to enhance my relationships."

2. Set Learning Objectives:

- o Define specific, measurable, achievable, relevant, and time-bound (SMART) objectives.
- o *Example:* "Complete a communication skills workshop within the next three months."

3. Create an Action Plan:

- o Outline the steps needed to achieve each learning objective.
- o *Example:* "Research available workshops, enroll in one by the end of the month, and attend all sessions."

4. Monitor Progress:

- o Regularly review your progress towards each objective.
- o *Example:* "Track attendance and apply learned techniques in daily interactions."

Purpose:

This plan ensures that you remain committed to your personal growth by continuously seeking new knowledge and skills, fostering adaptability and resilience.

Personal Insight:

Setting continuous learning goals has kept me engaged and motivated. It provides a clear roadmap for my personal development, ensuring that I remain proactive in my transformation journey.

Reflection Prompt:

What areas of personal growth do you wish to explore further? How can setting continuous learning goals support your sustained transformation?

2. Building and Maintaining Healthy Habits

Healthy habits form the backbone of sustained transformation. Establishing routines that promote physical, emotional, and spiritual well-being helps reinforce positive changes and prevent relapse into old patterns.

"And whatsoever ye do, do it heartily, as to the Lord, and not unto men." – **Colossians 3:23 (KJV)**

Practical Exercise: Habit Tracker

Instructions:

1. **Identify Key Habits:**

   o   List the habits you want to cultivate or maintain.
   o   *Example:* "Daily prayer, regular exercise, mindful eating."

2. **Set Clear Intentions:**

   o   Define what each habit entails and its purpose.
   o   *Example:* "Prayer: Spend 10 minutes each morning in prayer and scripture reading."

3. Create a Tracking System:

- o Use a journal, app, or calendar to monitor your habits.
- o *Example:* "Mark each day I complete my prayer time on a calendar."

4. Review and Adjust:

- o Regularly assess your habit tracker to identify patterns and areas for improvement.
- o *Example:* "If I miss a day of exercise, analyze why and adjust my schedule accordingly."

Purpose:

Tracking your habits increases accountability and provides visual evidence of your commitment, encouraging consistency and perseverance.

Personal Insight:

Using a habit tracker has significantly improved my ability to maintain daily practices. It offers a sense of accomplishment and motivates me to continue adhering to my routines.

Reflection Prompt:

Which habits are essential for sustaining your transformation? How can tracking these habits enhance your commitment to maintaining them?

3. Staying Connected with Your Support System

A robust support system plays a vital role in sustaining transformation. Regular interactions with supportive individuals provide encouragement, accountability, and a sense of community, all of which are essential for maintaining your growth.

"Bear ye one another's burdens, and so fulfil the law of Christ." – **Galatians 6:2 (KJV)**

Practical Exercise: Strengthening Support Connections

Instructions:

1. **List Your Supportive Contacts:**

   o Identify friends, family members, mentors, and community members who support your growth.
   o *Example:* "List three friends who offer emotional support, a mentor for spiritual guidance, and members of my church group."

2. **Schedule Regular Check-ins:**

   o Set up consistent times to connect with your support network.
   o *Example:* "Arrange a weekly phone call with my mentor and attend bi-weekly meetups with my church group."

3. Engage Actively:

- o Participate actively in your support interactions by sharing your progress and seeking advice.
- o *Example:* "Share my personal development goals during meetings and seek feedback on my progress."

4. Offer Support in Return:

- o Provide encouragement and assistance to others in your support system.
- o *Example:* "Offer to help a friend with their goals or provide prayer support during their challenges."

Purpose:

Maintaining strong connections with your support system fosters a sense of belonging and provides the necessary encouragement to persevere in your transformation journey.

Personal Insight:

Regularly engaging with my support network has been instrumental in sustaining my transformation. Their encouragement and accountability keep me motivated and focused on my goals.

Reflection Prompt:

How can you enhance your relationships within your support system to better sustain your transformation? What steps can you take to both receive and offer support?

4. Embracing Spiritual Practices

Spiritual practices anchor your transformation in faith, providing guidance, strength, and a sense of purpose. Regular engagement with spiritual disciplines reinforces your commitment to growth and aligns your actions with your beliefs.

"But they that wait upon the LORD shall renew their strength; they shall mount up with wings as eagles; they shall run, and not be weary; and they shall walk, and not faint." – **Isaiah 40:31 (KJV)**

Practical Exercise: Developing a Spiritual Routine

Instructions:

1. **Identify Spiritual Practices:**

   o   Determine the spiritual disciplines that resonate with you and support your growth.

   o   *Example:* "Daily prayer, scripture reading, meditation, worship music."

2. **Set a Schedule:**

   o   Allocate specific times for each spiritual practice in your daily or weekly routine.

o *Example:* "Morning prayer and scripture reading for 15 minutes, evening meditation for 10 minutes."

3. Create a Sacred Space:

o Designate a physical space in your home for your spiritual practices, free from distractions.
o *Example:* "Set up a small prayer corner with a Bible, a journal, and calming decor."

4. Reflect and Adjust:

o Regularly assess your spiritual routine to ensure it meets your needs and supports your growth.
o *Example:* "Evaluate the effectiveness of my meditation practice monthly and make adjustments as needed."

Purpose:

Establishing a consistent spiritual routine deepens your faith, provides clarity, and reinforces the values that drive your transformation.

Personal Insight:

Developing a dedicated spiritual routine has been transformative in my journey. It offers moments of reflection, strengthens my connection with God, and provides the spiritual nourishment needed to sustain my growth.

Reflection Prompt:

What spiritual practices can you incorporate into your daily life to support your sustained transformation? How can these practices enhance your connection with your faith and reinforce your personal growth?

5. Practicing Self-Compassion and Patience

Sustained transformation requires patience and self-compassion. Acknowledging that growth takes time and being kind to yourself during setbacks fosters resilience and a positive self-image.

"Be careful for nothing; but in every thing by prayer and supplication with thanksgiving let your requests be made known unto God." – **Philippians 4:6 (KJV)**

Practical Exercise: Self-Compassion Journal

Instructions:

1. **Create a Journal:**

   o Dedicate a notebook or digital document for self-compassion reflections.
   o *Example:* "Set up a separate section in my journal titled 'Self-Compassion.'"

2. **Daily Affirmations:**

   o Write down affirming statements that encourage self-kindness and patience.

o *Example:* "I am worthy of love and respect," "It's okay to take time to heal."

3. Reflect on Challenges:

o Acknowledge daily challenges and respond with compassion.

o *Example:* "Today, I felt overwhelmed by work. I choose to forgive myself and take a break."

4. Practice Gratitude:

o Incorporate gratitude entries to balance self-compassion with appreciation.

o *Example:* "I am grateful for the progress I've made and the lessons learned from my struggles."

Purpose:

This journal fosters a nurturing relationship with yourself, promoting emotional healing and sustained transformation through self-compassion and patience.

Personal Insight:

Maintaining a self-compassion journal has helped me navigate setbacks with grace and kindness. It reminds me to celebrate my progress and treat myself with the same love I offer to others.

Reflection Prompt:

How can you cultivate a more compassionate and patient attitude towards yourself during your transformation journey? What practices can support this mindset?

Maintaining Accountability

Accountability is a powerful tool for sustaining transformation. It involves taking responsibility for your actions, staying committed to your goals, and seeking feedback to ensure continued growth.

"For lack of counsel they are made waste: and without sharp sword they perish." – **Proverbs 11:14 (KJV)**

Practical Exercise: Accountability Check-ins

Instructions:

1. **Set Up Regular Check-ins:**

   o Schedule consistent times to review your progress with an accountability partner or group.
   o *Example:* "Arrange bi-weekly meetings with my accountability partner to discuss my goals and challenges."

2. **Define Accountability Goals:**

   o Clearly outline the aspects you want to stay accountable for.

o   *Example:* "Maintain my daily prayer routine, complete my personal development workshop, and track my exercise habits."

3. Prepare for Check-ins:

o   Reflect on your progress and prepare to share updates, challenges, and successes.

o   *Example:* "Prepare a brief summary of my achievements and areas needing improvement for each meeting."

4. Seek and Provide Feedback:

o   Engage in open and honest discussions, offering and receiving constructive feedback.

o   *Example:* "Listen actively to my partner's feedback and offer my own insights to help them in their journey."

Purpose:

Regular accountability check-ins keep you focused on your goals, provide external motivation, and offer opportunities for growth through feedback and support.

Personal Insight:

Engaging in accountability check-ins has been instrumental in maintaining my commitment to my goals. The mutual support and honest feedback from my accountability partner keep me aligned and motivated.

Reflection Prompt:

Who can you entrust as your accountability partner to support your sustained transformation? How can you structure your check-ins to maximize their effectiveness?

Embracing Flexibility and Adaptability

Sustaining transformation requires flexibility and adaptability. Life is unpredictable, and being able to adjust your plans and goals in response to changing circumstances ensures that your growth remains resilient and sustainable.

"And he that is void of wisdom despiseth his neighbour: but a man of understanding holdeth his peace." – **Proverbs 11:12 (KJV)**

Practical Exercise: Adaptability Planning

Instructions:

1. **Identify Potential Challenges:**

   o Anticipate obstacles that might disrupt your transformation journey.
   o *Example:* "Unexpected work commitments, health issues, or personal setbacks."

2. **Develop Contingency Plans:**

   o Outline strategies to address each potential challenge.

o *Example:* "If I face unexpected work commitments, I will adjust my exercise schedule to mornings instead of evenings."

3. Stay Open to Change:

o Embrace changes as opportunities for growth rather than threats.
o *Example:* "View a career change as a chance to develop new skills and broaden my experiences."

4. Reflect and Adjust:

o Regularly review your plans and make necessary adjustments to stay aligned with your goals.
o *Example:* "Monthly review sessions to assess the effectiveness of my contingency plans and make improvements."

Purpose:

This planning fosters a proactive approach to potential disruptions, ensuring that your transformation journey remains on track despite unforeseen changes.

Personal Insight:

Embracing flexibility has allowed me to navigate unexpected challenges without derailing my transformation. It teaches me to remain resilient and resourceful, adapting my strategies to maintain progress.

Reflection Prompt:

How can you cultivate a mindset of flexibility and adaptability in your transformation journey? What steps can you take to prepare for unexpected changes?

Nurturing Your Physical Well-being

Physical health is intrinsically linked to emotional and spiritual well-being. Maintaining a healthy lifestyle supports your transformation by providing the energy and vitality needed to pursue your goals.

"Or do you not know that your body is the temple of the Holy Ghost which is in you, which ye have of God, and ye are not your own?" – **1 Corinthians 6:19 (KJV)**

Practical Exercise: Holistic Health Plan

Instructions:

1. **Assess Your Current Health:**

   o Evaluate your physical health, identifying areas that need improvement.
   o *Example:* "Assess my current exercise routine, diet, and sleep patterns."

2. **Set Health Goals:**

   o Define specific, achievable goals related to your physical well-being.

o   *Example:* "Incorporate 30 minutes of exercise into my daily routine and maintain a balanced diet rich in fruits and vegetables."

3. Create a Wellness Schedule:

o   Develop a schedule that includes exercise, healthy eating, and adequate rest.

o   *Example:* "Exercise every morning, prepare healthy meals in advance, and ensure <u>7-8 hours</u> of sleep each night."

4. Monitor Progress:

o   Track your health-related activities and progress towards your goals.

o   *Example:* "Use a fitness app to log workouts and monitor nutritional intake."

Purpose:

This plan promotes a balanced and healthy lifestyle, providing the physical foundation necessary for sustained transformation and personal growth.

Personal Insight:

Prioritizing my physical health has had a profound impact on my overall well-being. Regular exercise and a nutritious diet boost my energy levels, enhance my mood, and support my spiritual practices, contributing to a holistic transformation.

Reflection Prompt:

What aspects of your physical health can you improve to support your sustained transformation? How can implementing a holistic health plan enhance your overall well-being?

Cultivating a Growth Mindset

A growth mindset is essential for sustaining transformation. It involves believing in your ability to grow, embracing challenges, and viewing failures as opportunities for learning and development.

"For lack of counsel they are made waste: and without sharp sword they perish." – **Proverbs 11:14 (KJV)**

Practical Exercise: Growth Mindset Affirmations

Instructions:

1. **Identify Limiting Beliefs:**

   o Recognize thoughts that hinder your growth and transformation.
   o *Example:* "I am not capable of achieving my goals."

2. **Develop Affirmations:**

   o Create positive statements that counteract your limiting beliefs.

  o *Example:* "I am capable of achieving my goals through dedication and faith."

3. Daily Repetition:

  o Recite your affirmations daily, ideally in the morning and evening.

  o *Example:* "Every morning, affirm my capabilities and every evening, reflect on my progress."

4. Visualize Success:

  o Pair your affirmations with visualization techniques to reinforce your belief in your growth.

  o *Example:* "Visualize yourself successfully completing a challenging project while reciting your affirmations."

Purpose:

Affirmations foster a positive and resilient mindset, encouraging continuous growth and the ability to overcome obstacles.

Personal Insight:

Incorporating growth mindset affirmations has shifted my perspective from seeing challenges as insurmountable to viewing them as opportunities for development. This shift has been instrumental in maintaining my transformation journey.

Reflection Prompt:

What limiting beliefs do you need to address to sustain your transformation? How can affirmations and visualization support the cultivation of a growth mindset?

Leveraging Technology for Growth

In the digital age, technology can be a valuable ally in sustaining transformation. Utilizing apps, online communities, and digital resources can enhance your personal growth efforts by providing tools for tracking, learning, and connecting.

"And whatsoever ye do, do it heartily, as to the Lord, and not unto men." – **Colossians 3:23 (KJV)**

Practical Exercise: Digital Tools for Personal Growth

Instructions:

1. **Identify Useful Apps and Resources:**

   o Research and select apps that support your personal growth goals.

   o *Example:* "Use a meditation app like Headspace, a fitness tracker like Fitbit, and a journaling app like Day One."

2. Integrate Technology into Your Routine:

o   Incorporate these digital tools into your daily practices to enhance consistency and accountability.

o   *Example:* "Set reminders on my phone to meditate and track my workouts using the fitness app."

3. Engage with Online Communities:

o   Join online forums, social media groups, or virtual workshops that align with your growth objectives.

o   *Example:* "Participate in an online Bible study group or a personal development webinar."

4. Utilize Educational Platforms:

o   Enroll in online courses or access digital libraries to continue your learning journey.

o   *Example:* "Take an online course on emotional intelligence to improve my interpersonal skills."

Purpose:

Leveraging technology provides accessible and convenient ways to support your personal growth, offering tools that enhance your practices and connect you with a broader community.

Personal Insight:

Integrating technology into my transformation journey has streamlined my efforts, making it easier to track progress, stay motivated, and access resources that support my growth.

Reflection Prompt:

How can you utilize technology to support your sustained transformation? What digital tools or online communities can enhance your personal growth journey?

Balancing Ambition with Contentment

While striving for continuous growth, it's essential to balance ambition with contentment. Recognizing and appreciating your progress prevents burnout and fosters a sense of fulfillment, ensuring that your transformation remains sustainable.

"The heart of the righteous studieth to answer: but the mouth of the wicked poureth out evil things." – **Proverbs 15:28 (KJV)**

Practical Exercise: Contentment Reflection

Instructions:

1. **List Your Achievements:**

   o   Write down the goals you've achieved and the progress you've made.

o *Example:* "Completed a personal development workshop, established a daily prayer routine, improved my physical fitness."

2. **Express Gratitude:**

o Reflect on the positive changes and express gratitude for your accomplishments.

o *Example:* "I am grateful for the dedication that allowed me to complete my workshop and for the support of my accountability partner."

3. **Set Realistic Expectations:**

o Ensure that your goals are achievable and align with your current life circumstances.

o *Example:* "Set a goal to read one book per month instead of four to maintain balance."

4. **Celebrate Milestones:**

o Acknowledge and celebrate your achievements, no matter how small.

o *Example:* "Treat myself to a special meal or a day of relaxation after reaching a milestone."

Purpose:

This reflection fosters a sense of fulfillment and appreciation for your journey, preventing the tendency to overextend and ensuring that your transformation remains enjoyable and sustainable.

Personal Insight:

Balancing ambition with contentment has been pivotal in my transformation journey. It allows me to strive for growth while appreciating the progress I've made, maintaining motivation without succumbing to burnout.

Reflection Prompt:

How can you cultivate a sense of contentment while continuing to pursue personal growth? What practices can help you appreciate your achievements and maintain balance in your transformation journey?

Embracing Forgiveness and Letting Go

Sustained transformation involves letting go of past hurts, grudges, and negative emotions that hinder your growth. Embracing forgiveness liberates you from emotional baggage, allowing you to move forward with a clear and focused mind.

"And be ye kind one to another, tenderhearted, forgiving one another, even as God for Christ's sake hath forgiven you." – **Ephesians 4:32 (KJV)**

Practical Exercise: Forgiveness Ritual

Instructions:

1. **Identify Areas for Forgiveness:**

   o   Reflect on individuals or situations where you hold resentment or negative emotions.

- o *Example:* "Forgive a family member who betrayed my trust."

2. **Acknowledge Your Emotions:**

   - o Recognize and validate the feelings associated with the hurt.
   - o *Example:* "Acknowledge feelings of anger and sadness towards the person who hurt me."

3. **Seek Divine Guidance:**

   - o Pray for the strength and wisdom to forgive.
   - o *Example:* "Pray for the ability to release resentment and embrace forgiveness."

4. **Perform the Forgiveness:**

   - o Make a conscious decision to forgive, either through prayer, writing a letter (even if you don't send it), or a symbolic gesture.
   - o *Example:* "Write a forgiveness letter and read it aloud to symbolize letting go."

5. **Reflect on the Process:**

   - o Consider how forgiveness has impacted your emotional and spiritual well-being.
   - o *Example:* "Journal about the feelings of relief and peace after performing the forgiveness ritual."

Purpose:

This ritual promotes emotional healing and frees you from the burdens of past hurts, fostering a positive and open mindset essential for sustained transformation.

Personal Insight:

Engaging in forgiveness rituals has been profoundly liberating. It has allowed me to release pent-up emotions and focus on my growth without the weight of past grievances holding me back.

Reflection Prompt:

What steps can you take to forgive past hurts and let go of negative emotions? How can forgiveness enhance your ability to sustain your transformation?

Integrating Spiritual Accountability

Spiritual accountability involves seeking guidance and support from your faith community or spiritual mentors. It provides a framework for maintaining your spiritual health and ensuring that your transformation aligns with your faith values.

"Iron sharpeneth iron; so a man sharpeneth the countenance of his friend." – **Proverbs 27:17 (KJV)**

Practical Exercise: Spiritual Accountability Partnership

Instructions:

1. **Identify a Spiritual Accountability Partner:**

   o Choose a trusted individual within your faith community or mentorship network.

   o *Example:* "Partner with a fellow church member who shares similar spiritual goals."

2. **Set Clear Expectations:**

   o Define the nature and frequency of your accountability interactions.

   o *Example:* "Meet monthly to discuss our spiritual journeys and offer mutual support."

3. **Share Your Spiritual Goals:**

   o Communicate your goals and the areas where you seek accountability.

   o *Example:* "Share my goal to deepen my prayer life and seek guidance on maintaining consistency."

4. **Provide and Receive Support:**

   o Engage in honest and open discussions, offering encouragement and constructive feedback.

   o *Example:* "Encourage each other to stay committed to our prayer routines and celebrate milestones together."

5. Pray Together:

- o Incorporate prayer into your accountability meetings, seeking divine guidance and strength.
- o *Example:* "Start each meeting with a prayer for mutual growth and support."

Purpose:

This partnership fosters spiritual growth and ensures that your transformation journey remains aligned with your faith, providing a supportive and encouraging environment for sustained change.

Personal Insight:

Having a spiritual accountability partner has been invaluable in my transformation journey. Their encouragement and shared faith goals provide a sense of direction and motivation, keeping me aligned with my spiritual aspirations.

Reflection Prompt:

Who can you entrust as your spiritual accountability partner to support your sustained transformation? How can you structure your partnership to maximize its effectiveness?

Embracing Rest and Renewal

Sustained transformation requires periods of rest and renewal. Taking time to rest prevents burnout, rejuvenates your spirit, and ensures that you remain energized and motivated in your journey.

"Come unto me, all ye that labour and are heavy laden, and I will give you rest." – **Matthew 11:28 (KJV)**

Practical Exercise: Rest and Renewal Schedule

Instructions:

1. **Identify Rest Activities:**

   o Determine activities that help you relax and rejuvenate.
   o *Example:* "Read a book, take a nature walk, meditate, engage in hobbies."

2. **Set Rest Periods:**

   o Allocate specific times in your schedule for rest and relaxation.
   o *Example:* "Dedicate Sunday afternoons to leisure activities and self-care."

3. **Create a Relaxation Routine:**

   o Develop a routine that includes regular breaks and downtime.
   o *Example:* "Incorporate a 10-minute meditation break every afternoon to reset and recharge."

4. Monitor Your Energy Levels:

o   Pay attention to your energy and stress levels, adjusting your schedule as needed to include sufficient rest.

o   *Example:* "If I feel overwhelmed, take an additional short break to prevent burnout."

Purpose:

This schedule ensures that you prioritize rest and renewal, maintaining your physical, emotional, and spiritual well-being essential for sustained transformation.

Personal Insight:

Incorporating regular rest periods into my routine has significantly enhanced my productivity and overall well-being. It allows me to return to my goals with renewed energy and a clear mind.

Reflection Prompt:

How can you incorporate regular periods of rest and renewal into your daily or weekly routine? What activities help you relax and recharge?

Leveraging Reflection and Self-Assessment

Regular reflection and self-assessment are critical for sustaining transformation. They allow you to evaluate your progress, recognize achievements, identify areas for improvement, and realign your goals with your evolving aspirations.

"Examine yourselves, whether ye be in the faith; prove your own selves." – **2 Corinthians 13:5 (KJV)**

Practical Exercise: Monthly Self-Assessment

Instructions:

1. **Set Aside Reflection Time:**

   o   Allocate a specific time each month for self-assessment.
   o   *Example:* "Schedule the last Sunday of each month for a self-assessment session."

2. **Review Your Goals and Progress:**

   o   Evaluate how well you've met your personal growth goals.
   o   *Example:* "Assess whether I've maintained my daily prayer routine and identify any obstacles faced."

3. **Identify Achievements and Challenges:**

   o   Celebrate your successes and acknowledge the challenges encountered.
   o   *Example:* "Celebrate completing my meditation course and reflect on the difficulties in maintaining a balanced diet."

4. Adjust Your Goals and Strategies:

- o Modify your goals and strategies based on your self-assessment findings.
- o *Example:* "If maintaining a balanced diet has been challenging, seek nutritional guidance or adjust meal planning techniques."

5. Set New Objectives:

- o Define new goals to continue your personal growth journey.
- o *Example:* "Set a new goal to volunteer regularly in my community to enhance my sense of purpose."

Purpose:

This self-assessment fosters continuous improvement, ensuring that your transformation journey remains dynamic and aligned with your evolving goals and circumstances.

Personal Insight:

Engaging in regular self-assessments has provided me with clarity and direction. It helps me recognize my progress, address areas needing attention, and set new objectives that keep me motivated and committed to my growth.

Reflection Prompt:

How can regular self-assessments enhance your sustained transformation? What questions can you ask yourself during these assessments to gain deeper insights into your progress?

Embracing Gratitude and Positivity

Cultivating an attitude of gratitude and maintaining a positive outlook are essential for sustaining transformation. Gratitude shifts your focus from what you lack to what you have, fostering contentment and enhancing your overall well-being.

"Rejoice evermore. Pray without ceasing. In every thing give thanks: for this is the will of God in Christ Jesus concerning you." – **1 Thessalonians 5:16-18 (KJV)**

Practical Exercise: Daily Gratitude Practice

Instructions:

1. **Choose Your Medium:**

   o   Select a journal, digital document, or gratitude app for your practice.
   o   *Example:* "Use my morning journal to list three things I'm grateful for each day."

2. **Set a Routine:**

   o   Dedicate a specific time each day for your gratitude practice.
   o   *Example:* "Write my gratitude list every morning after waking up."

3. Be Specific:

- o Focus on specific details rather than general statements to enhance the impact of your gratitude.
- o *Example:* "Instead of saying 'I'm grateful for my family,' specify 'I'm grateful for the support my sister provided during my difficult week.'"

4. Reflect on Your Entries:

- o Periodically review your gratitude entries to reinforce positive thinking and recognize patterns.
- o *Example:* "Read through my gratitude journal each month to appreciate the abundance in my life."

Purpose:

This practice fosters a positive mindset, enhances emotional well-being, and reinforces the progress you've made in your transformation journey.

Personal Insight:

Maintaining a daily gratitude practice has significantly improved my outlook on life. It helps me appreciate the small blessings and stay motivated to continue my personal growth efforts.

Reflection Prompt:

How can cultivating a daily gratitude practice support your sustained transformation? What specific things are you grateful for that align with your growth journey?

Conclusion: Embracing a Lifelong Journey of Transformation

Sustaining your transformation is a testament to your resilience, dedication, and unwavering commitment to personal growth. It involves continuous learning, maintaining healthy habits, leveraging your support system, engaging in spiritual practices, and fostering a positive and adaptable mindset. By integrating these strategies into your daily life, you ensure that your transformation remains dynamic, fulfilling, and aligned with your deepest values and faith.

"For I know the thoughts that I think toward you, saith the LORD, thoughts of peace, and not of evil, to give you an expected end." – **Jeremiah 29:11 (KJV)**

Final Prayer:

"Heavenly Father, thank You for the strength and wisdom You've provided throughout my transformation journey. Help me to sustain the growth I've achieved and remain committed to continuous improvement. Grant me the resilience to overcome challenges, the humility to seek support, and the faith to trust in Your divine guidance. May my transformation honor You and serve as a beacon of Your love and grace to those around me. In Jesus' name, Amen."

CHAPTER 10

Inspirational Tips for Integrating Faith Seamlessly

Introduction: Blending Faith with Daily Life

Integrating faith seamlessly into your daily life is a profound way to enhance your transformation journey. Faith acts as a guiding light, offering strength, purpose, and direction as you navigate the complexities of personal growth and healing. By weaving your spiritual beliefs into everyday activities, you create a harmonious balance that not only supports your transformation but also enriches your overall well-being. This chapter provides inspirational tips and practical strategies to help you incorporate faith into various aspects of your life, ensuring that your spiritual journey remains a central pillar in your pursuit of personal growth.

"Commit thy works unto the LORD, and thy thoughts shall be established." – **Proverbs 16:3 (KJV)**

Reflection Prompt:

Consider the ways in which your faith currently influences your daily activities. How can you deepen the integration of your spiritual beliefs into your everyday routines to support your personal growth and transformation?

1. Morning Devotionals: Starting Your Day with Faith

Beginning your day with a time of devotion sets a positive and purposeful tone, grounding you in your faith and preparing you for the challenges ahead. Morning devotionals can include prayer, scripture reading, and reflection, fostering a strong spiritual foundation that supports your transformation throughout the day.

Practical Exercise: Establishing a Morning Devotional Routine

Instructions:

1. **Choose a Consistent Time:**

   Select a specific time each morning dedicated to your devotional practice. Consistency helps in forming a lasting habit.
   Example: "Wake up 30 minutes earlier to spend time in prayer and scripture reading."

2. Create a Sacred Space:

Designate a quiet and comfortable area in your home where you can focus without distractions.
Example: "Set up a small table with a Bible, a journal, and a candle in my bedroom."

3. Select Devotional Materials:

Choose a devotional book or online resource that resonates with your spiritual journey.
Example: "Use a daily devotional guide that includes scripture, meditation prompts, and prayer points."

4. Incorporate Reflection and Journaling:

After reading scripture, take a few moments to reflect on its meaning and how it applies to your life.
Example: "Write down key insights and personal reflections in a journal to reinforce understanding."

5. Pray and Seek Guidance:

End your devotional time with prayer, seeking God's guidance and strength for the day ahead.
Example: "Pray for wisdom, patience, and the ability to embody the teachings of the scripture."

Purpose:

This routine anchors your day in faith, providing spiritual nourishment and clarity that supports your personal growth and transformation.

Personal Insight:

Incorporating morning devotionals into my daily routine has significantly enhanced my sense of purpose and direction. It serves as a spiritual reset, allowing me to approach each day with a clear mind and a focused heart.

Scriptural Reinforcement:

"Let the morning bring me word of thy lovingkindness, for I have hoped in thee: let me hear thy voice in the morning, for thou hast my goodly heritage." – **Psalm 143:8 (KJV)**

Reflection Prompt:

How can a morning devotional practice transform your approach to each day? What specific elements would you like to include to make your devotionals more meaningful and impactful?

2. Incorporating Scripture into Daily Activities

Embedding scripture into your daily tasks ensures that your faith remains present and influential throughout the day. Whether you're commuting, working, or engaging in leisure activities, integrating scripture can provide continuous spiritual guidance and encouragement.

Practical Exercise: Scripture Integration in Daily Activities

Instructions:

1. **Identify Key Activities:**

    List daily activities where you can incorporate scripture reading or memorization.
    Example: "Commuting to work, exercising, preparing meals."

2. **Choose Relevant Scriptures:**

    Select scriptures that align with the nature of each activity or your personal growth goals.
    Example: "During exercise, meditate on scriptures about strength and perseverance."

3. **Utilize Technology:**

    Use smartphone apps or audio recordings to access scriptures during activities.
    Example: "Listen to a daily scripture podcast while jogging."

4. **Set Reminders:**

    Schedule reminders on your phone to prompt scripture reading or reflection at specific times.
    Example: "Set a reminder to read a scripture before lunch each day."

5. Reflect and Apply:

Take moments during or after activities to reflect on the scriptures and consider their application in your life.
Example: "After preparing a meal, meditate on the scripture about provision and thankfulness."

Purpose:

Integrating scripture into daily activities keeps your faith at the forefront, providing ongoing inspiration and reinforcement of your spiritual values.

Personal Insight:

Incorporating scripture into my daily activities has created a seamless connection between my faith and everyday life. It ensures that spiritual growth is a constant and integrated part of my personal transformation.

Scriptural Reinforcement:

"I have set the LORD always before me: because he is at my right hand, I shall not be moved." – **Psalm 16:8 (KJV)**

Reflection Prompt:

Which daily activities can you enhance by integrating scripture? How can you make scripture reading a more organic and less forced part of your routine?

3. Mindful Prayer Practices: Connecting Throughout the Day

Prayer is a powerful tool for maintaining a connection with God, seeking guidance, and expressing gratitude. Mindful prayer practices can be seamlessly integrated into various moments of your day, fostering a continuous dialogue with the Divine.

Practical Exercise: Implementing Mindful Prayer Moments

Instructions:

1. **Identify Prayer Opportunities:**

   Recognize moments in your day where you can pause for prayer, such as before meals, during breaks, or before bedtime.
   Example: "Pray before each meal and during morning and evening breaks."

2. **Use Prayer Prompts:**

   Utilize specific prayer prompts to guide your prayers, ensuring they are meaningful and focused.
   Example: "Pray for strength, guidance, gratitude, and the well-being of loved ones."

3. **Keep a Prayer Journal:**

   Document your prayers and reflections in a journal to track your spiritual journey and growth.

Example: "Write down prayer requests and note any answered prayers or insights gained."

4. Incorporate Breathing Techniques:

Combine prayer with deep breathing to enhance focus and relaxation.
Example: "Take deep breaths while reciting a prayer to calm the mind and center the spirit."

5. Join Prayer Groups:

Participate in group prayers or prayer chains to foster a sense of community and collective faith.
Example: "Attend a weekly prayer meeting at church or join an online prayer group."

Purpose:

Mindful prayer practices ensure that your connection with God remains active and vibrant throughout the day, providing spiritual sustenance and support for your transformation journey.

Personal Insight:

Integrating prayer into my daily routine has deepened my relationship with God and provided a constant source of comfort and guidance. It serves as a spiritual anchor, keeping me grounded and focused amidst life's demands.

Scriptural Reinforcement:

"Pray without ceasing." – **1 Thessalonians 5:17 (KJV)**

Reflection Prompt:

How can you make prayer a more consistent and integrated part of your daily routine? What specific prayer practices resonate most with your personal growth and transformation?

4. Faith-Based Reflection and Meditation

Reflection and meditation on faith-related topics can significantly enhance your spiritual awareness and personal growth. These practices encourage deep thinking about your beliefs, values, and the ways in which faith influences your actions and decisions.

Practical Exercise: Faith-Based Reflection Sessions

Instructions:

1. **Schedule Reflection Time:**

   Allocate specific times each week for reflection and meditation on faith-related topics.
   Example: "Set aside one hour every Sunday afternoon for spiritual reflection."

2. Choose Reflection Themes:

Select themes or questions that encourage deep thinking about your faith and its role in your life.
Example: "Reflect on how faith has influenced my personal growth and decision-making."

3. Use Guided Meditations:

Utilize guided meditation resources that focus on faith and spiritual growth.
Example: "Listen to a guided Christian meditation that explores themes of forgiveness and renewal."

4. Incorporate Scripture:

Base your reflections and meditations on specific scripture passages to provide a spiritual framework.
Example: "Meditate on Psalm 1:1-3 and reflect on the blessings of righteous living."

5. Document Insights:

Write down your thoughts, feelings, and any insights gained during your reflection sessions.
Example: "Journal about how a particular scripture passage has inspired a change in my behavior or attitude."

Purpose:

Faith-based reflection and meditation deepen your spiritual understanding and foster personal growth by encouraging introspection and alignment with your faith values.

Personal Insight:

Engaging in regular reflection sessions has enhanced my spiritual awareness and provided clarity on my personal growth objectives. It allows me to align my actions with my faith, ensuring that my transformation is both meaningful and sustained.

Scriptural Reinforcement:

"But his delight is in the law of the LORD; and in his law doth he meditate day and night." – **Psalm 1:2 (KJV)**

Reflection Prompt:

What faith-related topics resonate most with your personal growth journey? How can you structure your reflection sessions to maximize their impact on your transformation?

5. Faith in Relationships: Cultivating Spiritual Connections

Integrating faith into your relationships fosters deeper connections and mutual growth. It encourages shared values, spiritual support, and collective encouragement, enhancing both personal and relational transformation.

Practical Exercise: Building Faith-Based Relationships

Instructions:

1. **Seek Like-Minded Individuals:**

   Engage with individuals who share your faith and values, fostering relationships grounded in spiritual commonality.
   Example: "Join a church group or a faith-based community to meet like-minded individuals."

2. **Engage in Spiritual Conversations:**

   Initiate and participate in discussions about faith, spiritual experiences, and personal growth.
   Example: "Discuss a recent scripture passage with a friend and explore its application in your lives."

3. **Participate in Faith Activities Together:**

   Share in faith-based activities that promote spiritual bonding and collective growth.
   Example: "Attend worship services, prayer meetings, or faith retreats with friends and family."

4. **Support Each Other's Faith Journeys:**

   Encourage and uplift each other in your respective spiritual paths, offering support during challenges and celebrating successes together.

Example: "Pray together regularly and provide encouragement during times of struggle."

5. Practice Forgiveness and Grace:

Incorporate principles of forgiveness and grace in your relationships, fostering a nurturing and compassionate environment.

Example: "Extend forgiveness to a friend who has wronged you, following the teachings of Ephesians 4:32."

Purpose:

Cultivating spiritual connections within your relationships enhances your support system, fosters mutual growth, and ensures that your transformation is supported by a community of faith.

Personal Insight:

Building faith-based relationships has enriched my life by providing a network of support and shared spiritual experiences. These connections offer encouragement and accountability, strengthening my commitment to personal growth and transformation.

Scriptural Reinforcement:

"And let us consider one another to provoke unto love and to good works." – **Hebrews 10:24 (KJV)**

Reflection Prompt:

How can you deepen the integration of faith within your existing relationships? What steps can you take to foster spiritual connections that support your personal growth and transformation?

6. Faith-Focused Goal Setting

Setting goals that align with your faith ensures that your personal growth objectives are spiritually grounded and purposeful. Faith-focused goal setting integrates your spiritual aspirations with your personal and professional ambitions, creating a holistic approach to transformation.

Practical Exercise: Faith-Aligned Goal Setting

Instructions:

1. **Define Spiritual Goals:**

    Identify goals that reflect your faith and spiritual aspirations.
    Example: "Deepen my understanding of scripture and apply its teachings in daily life."

2. **Align Personal Goals with Faith:**

    Ensure that your personal and professional goals are in harmony with your spiritual values.
    Example: "Pursue a career that allows me to serve others and make a positive impact in my community."

3. **Set SMART Goals:**

Develop Specific, Measurable, Achievable, Relevant, and Time-bound goals that incorporate your faith.

Example: "Read and study one chapter of the Bible each week for the next year."

4. **Create an Action Plan:**

Outline the steps needed to achieve each faith-aligned goal.

Example: "Join a Bible study group, set aside daily time for scripture reading, and attend weekly worship services."

5. **Monitor and Reflect:**

Regularly review your progress towards your goals and reflect on how they are influencing your spiritual growth.

Example: "Evaluate my scripture study routine monthly and adjust as needed to stay committed."

Purpose:

Faith-focused goal setting ensures that your personal growth is intentional, spiritually grounded, and aligned with your divine purpose, fostering a meaningful and sustained transformation.

Personal Insight:

Aligning my goals with my faith has provided a clear sense of purpose and direction. It ensures that my personal ambitions contribute to my spiritual growth and align with my core values.

Scriptural Reinforcement:

"Commit thy works unto the LORD, and thy thoughts shall be established." – **Proverbs 16:3 (KJV)**

Reflection Prompt:

What are your spiritual aspirations, and how can they be integrated into your personal and professional goals? How does aligning your goals with your faith enhance your commitment to achieving them?

7. Faith in Work and Career: Purpose-Driven Professionalism

Integrating faith into your work and career brings purpose and fulfillment to your professional life. It encourages ethical behavior, fosters a sense of calling, and ensures that your career aligns with your spiritual values and personal growth objectives.

Practical Exercise: Purpose-Driven Professionalism

Instructions:

1. **Identify Your Calling:**

   Reflect on how your career aligns with your faith and spiritual values.
   Example: "Determine how my role in healthcare serves others and reflects my commitment to compassion and service."

2. **Set Ethical Standards:**

   Establish ethical guidelines that reflect your spiritual beliefs and ensure integrity in your professional life.
   Example: "Commit to honesty, fairness, and respect in all my professional interactions."

3. **Seek Opportunities for Service:**

   Look for ways to serve others through your work, whether through mentorship, volunteer initiatives, or community engagement.
   Example: "Volunteer to lead a wellness workshop for underprivileged communities through my workplace."

4. **Incorporate Faith into Decision-Making:**

   Base your professional decisions on your spiritual values and seek divine guidance in your career choices.

Example: "Pray for wisdom when faced with difficult decisions and ensure they align with my faith."

5. Balance Work and Spiritual Life:

Maintain a healthy balance between your professional responsibilities and spiritual practices to prevent burnout and ensure holistic growth.
Example: "Set boundaries to ensure time for daily prayer and scripture reading, even during busy work periods."

Purpose:

Integrating faith into your work cultivates a sense of purpose and fulfillment, ensuring that your professional life contributes positively to your personal growth and aligns with your spiritual values.

Personal Insight:

Embracing faith in my career has transformed my approach to work, making it a platform for service and ethical practice. It provides a sense of fulfillment and ensures that my professional endeavors contribute to my overall transformation.

Scriptural Reinforcement:

"And whatsoever ye do, do it heartily, as to the Lord, and not unto men." – **Colossians 3:23 (KJV)**

Reflection Prompt:

How can you incorporate your faith into your professional life to enhance your sense of purpose and fulfillment? What steps can you take to ensure that your career aligns with your spiritual values?

8. Faith-Based Community Engagement

Engaging with your faith-based community fosters a sense of belonging and collective growth. It provides opportunities for service, shared experiences, and mutual support, enhancing both your personal transformation and that of others within the community.

Practical Exercise: Active Community Participation

Instructions:

1. **Join Faith-Based Organizations:**

   Become an active member of churches, prayer groups, or faith-based volunteer organizations.
   Example: "Volunteer with the church's outreach program to support local homeless shelters."

2. **Participate in Community Events:**

   Attend and contribute to events that promote faith and community building, such as retreats, seminars, and charity drives.

Example: "Participate in a church retreat focused on spiritual growth and personal development."

3. **Lead or Facilitate Groups:**

Take on leadership roles within your community to guide and support others in their faith and personal growth journeys.
Example: "Lead a weekly Bible study group to foster collective learning and spiritual discussion."

4. **Collaborate on Service Projects:**

Work with others in your community to organize and execute service projects that address local needs and promote collective well-being.
Example: "Organize a community clean-up day to beautify local parks and foster a spirit of cooperation."

5. **Foster Inclusivity and Diversity:**

Embrace and promote diversity within your community, ensuring that all members feel welcome and valued.
Example: "Encourage participation from individuals of various backgrounds in community events to enrich collective experiences."

Purpose:

Faith-based community engagement strengthens your support network, fosters mutual growth, and provides opportunities for service and collective transformation.

Personal Insight:

Active participation in my faith-based community has deepened my sense of belonging and provided numerous opportunities for service and personal growth. It reinforces the principles of compassion, collaboration, and mutual support that are essential for sustained transformation.

Scriptural Reinforcement:

"And let us consider one another to provoke unto love and to good works." – **Hebrews 10:24 (KJV)**

Reflection Prompt:

In what ways can you actively contribute to your faith-based community to support both your personal growth and the growth of others? What roles or activities resonate most with your skills and passions?

9. Faith-Integrated Self-Care Practices

Self-care is essential for maintaining physical, emotional, and spiritual well-being, which are crucial for sustaining transformation. Integrating faith into your self-care practices ensures that your efforts to nurture yourself are aligned with your spiritual values and personal growth objectives.

Practical Exercise: Faith-Integrated Self-Care Plan

Instructions:

1. **Identify Self-Care Activities:**

   Determine activities that promote your well-being and can be infused with your faith.
   Example: "Exercise while listening to worship music, engage in prayerful meditation, and enjoy nature walks as forms of spiritual renewal."

2. **Set a Self-Care Schedule:**

   Allocate specific times for self-care activities in your daily or weekly routine.
   Example: "Dedicate 30 minutes each evening to a spiritual meditation walk."

3. **Incorporate Faith Elements:**

   Infuse your self-care activities with faith-based elements to enhance their spiritual significance.
   Example: "Recite a favorite scripture verse during yoga sessions or meditate on God's promises while journaling."

4. **Create a Self-Care Ritual:**

   Develop a consistent ritual that combines self-care with spiritual practices.
   Example: "Begin each day with a cup of tea, a scripture reading, and a few moments of gratitude."

5. Reflect on Self-Care Benefits:

Regularly assess how your self-care practices are contributing to your overall well-being and transformation.

Example: "Journal about how prayerful meditation has improved my emotional resilience and spiritual clarity."

Purpose:

Integrating faith into self-care practices ensures that your efforts to nurture yourself are spiritually enriching and aligned with your personal growth goals, fostering holistic well-being.

Personal Insight:

Faith-integrated self-care has transformed how I approach my well-being. It turns self-care from a mere routine into a spiritually fulfilling practice that nurtures both my body and soul.

Scriptural Reinforcement:

"I will both lay me down in peace, and sleep: for thou, LORD, only makest me dwell in safety." – **Psalm 4:8 (KJV)**

Reflection Prompt:

How can you incorporate faith into your self-care practices to enhance both your physical and spiritual well-being? What specific activities can you integrate with your spiritual routines to nurture your overall health?

10. Faith in Decision-Making: Guided by Divine Wisdom

Incorporating faith into your decision-making process ensures that your choices are aligned with your spiritual values and personal growth objectives. It provides divine guidance, clarity, and assurance as you navigate life's complexities.

Practical Exercise: Faith-Guided Decision-Making Process

Instructions:

1. **Seek Divine Guidance:**

    Begin each decision-making process with prayer, seeking wisdom and clarity from God.
    Example: "Pray for discernment and understanding before making any significant decisions."

2. **Reflect on Scripture:**

    Consult relevant scriptures that offer guidance and principles related to your decision.
    Example: "Meditate on Proverbs 3:5-6 when facing a major career choice."

3. **Evaluate Alignment with Faith Values:**

Assess how each option aligns with your spiritual beliefs and personal values.
Example: "Consider whether a particular job opportunity aligns with my values of service and integrity."

4. **Seek Counsel:**

Consult with trusted spiritual mentors or advisors who can provide insights and support based on their understanding of your faith journey.
Example: "Discuss my decision with my pastor or a trusted mentor to gain their perspective."

5. **Listen to Your Inner Conviction:**

Pay attention to your intuition and the peace or unease you feel about each option, trusting that your faith will guide you toward the right choice.
Example: "Choose the option that feels aligned with my sense of purpose and inner peace."

6. **Make the Decision with Confidence:**

After thorough prayer, reflection, and consultation, make your decision confidently, trusting in God's plan for your life.
Example: "Choose to pursue further education in a field that feels called and supported by my community."

Purpose:

This process ensures that your decisions are spiritually informed and aligned with your faith, fostering choices that support your personal growth and transformation.

Personal Insight:

Incorporating faith into my decision-making has provided me with a sense of peace and assurance, knowing that my choices are guided by divine wisdom and aligned with my spiritual values.

Scriptural Reinforcement:

"Trust in the LORD with all thine heart; and lean not unto thine own understanding. In all thy ways acknowledge him, and he shall direct thy paths." – **Proverbs 3:5-6 (KJV)**

Reflection Prompt:

How can you incorporate faith into your decision-making processes to ensure that your choices align with your spiritual values and personal growth objectives? What steps can you take to seek divine guidance in your decisions?

11. Faith-Infused Goal Tracking and Evaluation

Tracking and evaluating your goals through the lens of faith ensures that your personal growth objectives remain aligned with your spiritual journey. It provides an opportunity to celebrate achievements, seek divine guidance for challenges, and realign your goals with your evolving faith and values.

Practical Exercise: Faith-Infused Goal Tracker

Instructions:

1. **Set Faith-Aligned Goals:**

   Define goals that reflect both your personal growth aspirations and your spiritual values.
   Example: "Increase my community service hours while deepening my prayer life."

2. **Create a Tracking System:**

   Develop a system to monitor your progress, incorporating faith-based reflections and scriptures.
   Example: "Use a journal to log daily prayer times and weekly community service activities."

3. **Incorporate Spiritual Milestones:**

   Include spiritual milestones in your goal tracking to measure both personal and spiritual growth.
   Example: "Achieve a consistent daily prayer routine and complete a service project each month."

4. **Reflect on Progress:**

   Regularly review your progress, reflecting on how your faith has influenced your growth and identifying areas for improvement.

Example: "Monthly reflection sessions to assess how prayer has impacted my community service efforts."

5. Seek Divine Feedback:

Pray for feedback and insights on your progress, allowing your faith to guide your evaluations and adjustments.

Example: "Ask for God's guidance on how to better integrate faith into my daily activities."

Purpose:

This goal tracking and evaluation system ensures that your personal growth remains spiritually grounded and aligned with your faith, fostering a harmonious and fulfilling transformation journey.

Personal Insight:

Faith-infused goal tracking has enhanced my ability to stay committed to my objectives while maintaining a strong connection to my spiritual values. It provides a balanced approach to measuring progress and seeking divine guidance.

Scriptural Reinforcement:

"Commit thy works unto the LORD, and thy thoughts shall be established." – **Proverbs 16:3 (KJV)**

Reflection Prompt:

How can tracking your goals through the lens of faith enhance your personal growth and transformation? What methods can you implement to ensure that your goal evaluations remain spiritually informed and aligned with your faith?

12. Embracing Faith-Based Learning and Growth Opportunities

Continuous learning and growth are essential for sustaining transformation. Engaging in faith-based learning opportunities enriches your spiritual knowledge and supports your personal development, ensuring that your transformation journey remains dynamic and evolving.

Practical Exercise: Engaging in Faith-Based Learning

Instructions:

1. **Enroll in Faith-Based Courses:**

   Participate in courses or workshops that focus on spiritual growth and personal development.
   Example: "Join a Christian leadership seminar to enhance my skills and deepen my faith."

2. **Read Faith-Enriched Literature:**

   Incorporate reading materials that blend spiritual insights with personal growth principles.

Example: "Read books by Christian authors that explore themes of forgiveness, resilience, and purpose."

3. Attend Faith Conferences and Seminars:

Participate in conferences and seminars that offer opportunities for learning, networking, and spiritual enrichment.

Example: "Attend an annual Christian personal development conference to connect with like-minded individuals and gain new insights."

4. Engage in Online Learning Communities:

Join online forums, webinars, and discussion groups that focus on faith and personal growth.

Example: "Participate in an online Bible study group that discusses practical applications of scripture in daily life."

5. Seek Mentorship and Guidance:

Find mentors who can provide guidance and share their experiences in integrating faith with personal growth.

Example: "Establish a mentorship relationship with a seasoned Christian leader who can offer advice and support."

Purpose:

Engaging in faith-based learning opportunities fosters continuous spiritual and personal growth, ensuring that your transformation journey remains informed, enriched, and aligned with your faith.

Personal Insight:

Participating in faith-based learning has expanded my understanding of how to integrate spiritual principles into my personal growth efforts. It provides a rich source of inspiration and practical strategies for sustaining transformation.

Scriptural Reinforcement:

"An intelligent heart acquires knowledge; and the ear of the wise seeketh knowledge." – **Proverbs 18:15 (KJV)**

Reflection Prompt:

What faith-based learning opportunities can you pursue to enhance your personal growth and transformation? How can these learning experiences deepen your spiritual understanding and support your ongoing journey?

13. Faith in Leisure: Harmonizing Rest and Spirituality

Leisure activities provide essential rest and relaxation, contributing to overall well-being and sustained transformation. Infusing leisure with faith ensures that your downtime is spiritually enriching and aligned with your personal growth objectives.

Practical Exercise: Faith-Infused Leisure Activities

Instructions:

1. **Identify Leisure Activities:**

   List activities that you enjoy and that promote relaxation and joy.
   Example: "Reading, hiking, painting, listening to music."

2. **Incorporate Spiritual Elements:**

   Integrate faith-based components into your leisure activities to enhance their spiritual significance.
   Example: "Read faith-based books during leisure time, hike in nature while meditating on scripture, paint scenes inspired by biblical stories."

3. **Schedule Regular Leisure Time:**

   Allocate specific times for leisure activities in your weekly schedule to ensure consistent rest and rejuvenation.
   Example: "Set aside Saturday afternoons for nature walks and reflection on Psalm 19:1."

4. **Combine Social and Spiritual Engagement:**

Engage in leisure activities with others who share your faith, fostering both social connections and spiritual growth.
Example: "Organize a Bible study picnic with friends to combine fellowship with leisure."

5. **Reflect on Leisure and Spirituality:**

After engaging in leisure activities, take moments to reflect on how these experiences have enriched your spiritual life and personal growth.
Example: "Journal about the peace and insights gained from a peaceful evening of reading and prayer."

Purpose:

Integrating faith into leisure activities ensures that your rest and relaxation are spiritually fulfilling and contribute to your overall well-being and transformation.

Personal Insight:

Infusing my leisure time with faith-based elements has transformed my relaxation into opportunities for spiritual renewal and reflection. It enhances the quality of my leisure experiences, making them more meaningful and aligned with my personal growth journey.

Scriptural Reinforcement:

"It is vain for you to rise up early, to sit up late, to eat the bread of sorrows: for so he giveth his beloved sleep." — **Psalm 127:2 (KJV)**

Reflection Prompt:

How can you harmonize your leisure activities with your faith to enhance both relaxation and spiritual growth? What specific changes can you make to infuse your downtime with meaningful spiritual practices?

14. Faith in Challenges: Trusting Through Adversity

Facing challenges is an inevitable part of the transformation journey. Integrating faith into how you handle adversity fosters resilience, hope, and a deeper trust in divine providence, ensuring that obstacles become opportunities for growth rather than hindrances.

Practical Exercise: Faith-Focused Adversity Management

Instructions:

1. **Embrace a Faith-Based Perspective:**

   View challenges as opportunities to grow and deepen your faith rather than as setbacks.

Example: "Consider a job loss as a chance to explore new career paths that align more closely with my passions and faith."

2. Seek Comfort in Scripture:

Turn to scripture for solace, guidance, and strength during difficult times.
Example: "Meditate on Isaiah 41:10 when feeling overwhelmed by fear or uncertainty."

3. Pray for Strength and Guidance:

Use prayer as a means to seek divine assistance and clarity in navigating challenges.
Example: "Pray for the courage to face challenges and the wisdom to make sound decisions during trials."

4. Engage in Community Support:

Lean on your faith community for support, encouragement, and practical assistance.
Example: "Reach out to church members for prayer support and practical help during a personal crisis."

5. Reflect on Past Triumphs:

Recall previous challenges you've overcome with faith to bolster your confidence and resilience.
Example: "Reflect on how prayer and community support helped me navigate past difficulties, reinforcing my trust in God's plan."

Purpose:

Integrating faith into adversity management transforms challenges into opportunities for spiritual growth and personal development, fostering resilience and a deeper trust in divine providence.

Personal Insight:

Facing challenges with a faith-based approach has been transformative. It provides a sense of purpose and resilience, knowing that I am supported by a higher power and a community of believers during tough times.

Scriptural Reinforcement:

"And we know that all things work together for good to them that love God, to them who are the called according to his purpose." – **Romans 8:28 (KJV)**

Reflection Prompt:

How can you apply your faith to reframe and navigate the challenges you are currently facing? What specific scriptures or prayer practices can support you during these times of adversity?

15. Faith in Celebrations: Honoring Milestones with Gratitude

Celebrating milestones is an important aspect of the transformation journey, providing opportunities to acknowledge progress, express gratitude, and reinforce your commitment to personal growth. Integrating faith into celebrations adds a deeper sense of meaning and purpose, ensuring that your achievements are recognized as blessings and testimonies of divine support.

Practical Exercise: Faith-Based Celebration Rituals

Instructions:

1. **Identify Milestones:**

   Determine significant achievements and milestones in your personal growth and transformation journey. *Example:* "Achieve a major career goal, complete a personal development course, or overcome a significant fear."

2. **Plan Faith-Infused Celebrations:**

   Organize celebrations that incorporate elements of your faith, such as prayer, scripture reading, and expressions of gratitude.
   Example: "Host a gratitude dinner with family and friends, including a prayer of thanks and a reading of Psalms."

3. **Express Gratitude to God:**

   Use celebrations as opportunities to thank God for His guidance, support, and blessings throughout your journey.

Example: "Begin a celebration with a prayer thanking God for the strength and wisdom that led to your achievement."

4. Share Your Testimony:

Share your experiences and the role of faith in your transformation journey with others during celebrations.
Example: "Tell your story of overcoming challenges with faith during a celebration gathering."

5. Involve Your Community:

Invite your faith community to join in your celebrations, fostering a sense of collective joy and support.
Example: "Organize a community potluck to celebrate a collective achievement, such as completing a group service project."

Purpose:

Faith-based celebration rituals honor your achievements, express gratitude, and reinforce the role of faith in your personal growth and transformation journey.

Personal Insight:

Integrating faith into my celebrations has added profound meaning to my achievements. It transforms celebrations from mere acknowledgments of success into heartfelt expressions of gratitude and testimonies of divine support.

Scriptural Reinforcement:

"Rejoice with them that do rejoice, and weep with them that weep." – **Romans 12:15 (KJV)**

Reflection Prompt:

How can you incorporate faith into your upcoming celebrations to honor your milestones with gratitude and purpose? What specific rituals or practices can you introduce to make your celebrations more spiritually meaningful?

Conclusion: Embracing a Faith-Enriched Transformation Journey

Integrating faith seamlessly into your daily life is a powerful way to sustain and enhance your transformation journey. By embedding spiritual practices into your routines, relationships, and personal growth efforts, you create a harmonious balance that supports your well-being and aligns your transformation with your divine purpose. Faith acts as both the foundation and the driving force behind your personal growth, providing strength, guidance, and a sense of meaning that transcends everyday challenges.

"For I know the thoughts that I think toward you, saith the LORD, thoughts of peace, and not of evil, to give you an expected end." – **Jeremiah 29:11 (KJV)**

Final Prayer for the Chapter:

"Heavenly Father, thank You for the guidance and strength You provide as I integrate my faith into every aspect of my life. Help me to blend my spiritual beliefs with my daily activities, fostering a harmonious and purposeful transformation journey. Grant me the wisdom to seek Your presence in all that I do and the grace to maintain a deep and abiding connection with You. May my transformation honor You and serve as a testament to Your unwavering support and love. In Jesus' name, Amen."

Next Steps: Continuing Your Journey Beyond the Book

While this book has provided you with a comprehensive guide to healing, sacrifice, and personal growth, your journey is far from over. Here are some next steps to ensure that your transformation continues to thrive:

1. **Stay Engaged with Community:**

   Remain active in your faith community, seeking opportunities for service, fellowship, and continued learning.

2. **Set New Goals:**

   As you achieve your initial goals, set new ones to maintain momentum and continue your personal growth journey.

3. **Seek Continuous Support:**

   Maintain your connections with your support system, mentors, and accountability partners to stay motivated and encouraged.

4. **Embrace Lifelong Learning:**

   Continue to seek knowledge and skills that enhance your personal and spiritual growth, staying open to new experiences and insights.

5. Share Your Story:

Inspire others by sharing your transformation journey, offering hope and encouragement to those who may be on similar paths.

Final Encouragement:

"Embrace each day as an opportunity for growth and healing. Let your heart remain open to the sacrifices that lead to profound personal transformation, and trust in the divine guidance that supports your journey. May your healing be deep, your growth continuous, and your faith steadfast."

Final Assurance

"Healing Hearts: Embracing Sacrifice for Personal Growth" has been a comprehensive guide designed to support your journey of healing, sacrifice, and transformation. Each chapter has been meticulously crafted to provide you with the tools, insights, and spiritual support necessary for sustained personal growth. As you move forward, carry these lessons with you, and continue to seek growth and healing through intentional sacrifice and unwavering faith. Your dedication to personal transformation is a testament to your strength and resilience, and with faith as your foundation, your journey will continue to be one of profound and lasting change.

ABOUT THE AUTHOR

Dr. Mark A. McConnell was born on February 7, 1963, and raised in Kansas City, Kansas, by devoted Christian parents. From a young age, his faith was central to his life, accepting Christ at the tender age of five. Dr. McConnell's foundational spiritual upbringing was nurtured at Mt. Zion Baptist Church under the guidance of Dr. C.L. Bachus.

He pursued higher education with a commitment to his calling, earning a Bachelor's degree in Religion and Philosophy from Bishop College in Dallas, Texas, in 1986. He continued his theological education, receiving a Master of Divinity from Midwestern Baptist Theological Seminary in Kansas City, Missouri, in 1989 and completing a Doctor of Theology (Th.D.) in May 2002.

Dr. McConnell has been blessed with a beautiful family. He married Paris McConnell, his steadfast partner and source of strength, on September 2, 1989. Together, they have three sons—Moses, Caleb, and Matthew—and are proud grandparents to Jayden and Jordan McConnell.

Answering the call to preach, Dr. McConnell delivered his first sermon in May 1984 and was ordained in August 1985. His pastoral journey has included leading three congregations: Southside First Baptist Church in Kansas City, Missouri; Prince of Peace Baptist Church in Peoria, Illinois; and currently, New Cornerstone Baptist Church in Peoria, Illinois. His service extends beyond the pulpit, having served two terms as Moderator of the Central Illinois Baptist District Association in Peoria, Illinois. His involvement with the Baptist General State Convention of Illinois spans over 31 years, during which he has held significant positions, including 2nd Vice President of both the Baptist General Congress of Christian Education and the Baptist General State Convention of Illinois.

Dr. McConnell's dedication and unwavering commitment have led to his current role as President of the Baptist General State Convention of Illinois. His passion for this esteemed body is evident in his consistent participation, having never missed a board meeting, annual session, or Congress of Christian Education. He firmly believes that God has positioned him to lead and serve, fostering unity and growth within the convention.

Dr. McConnell's vision is clear: to uphold and advance the legacy of the Baptist General State Convention of Illinois, continuing its history as a leading force among state conventions. Through dedication and collective effort, he is confident that this convention will remain a beacon of leadership, faith, and service.